T0125298

Inspiration and Insights from the World's Greatest Martial Artist

BRUCE LEE
ARTIST OF LIFE

edited by
John Little

TUTTLE Publishing
Tokyo | Rutland, Vermont | Singapore

Published by Tuttle Publishing, an imprint of Periplus Editions (HK) Ltd.

www.tuttlepublishing.com

Copyright © 2018 Bruce Lee Enterprises, LLC
First edition, 1999

ISBN 978-0-8048-5113-8

Library of Congress Cataloging-in-Publication Data

Lee. Bruce, 1940–1973.
Bruce Lee : artist of life/compiled and edited by John Little. — 1st pb ed.
xv, 269 p. : ill. ; 24 cm—(The Bruce Lee library : v. 6)
Includes bibliographical references (p. 263-264) and index.
ISBN 0-8048-3131-9 (hc) ISBN 0-8048-3263-3 (pb)
I. Lee, Bruce, 1940—1973. 2. Martial artists—United States Biography 3. Actors—United States Biography. I. Little, John R., 1960- . II. Title. III. Series: Lee, Bruce, 1940-1973. Bruce Lee library : v. 6.
GVIII3L44A3 1999
791.43'028'092—dc21
[B]   9933401
          CIP

Distributed by

North America, Latin America & Europe
Tuttle Publishing,
364 Innovation Drive
North Clarendon, VT. 05759-9436 U.S.A.
Tel: (802) 773-8930;
Fax: (802) 773-6993
info@tuttlepublishing.com
www.tuttlepublishing.com

Japan
Tuttle Publishing
Yaekari Building, 3rd Floor;
5-4-12 Osaki, Shinagawa-ku
Tokyo 141 0032
Tel: (81) 3 5437-0171;
Fax: (81) 3 5437-0755
sales@tuttle.co.jp
www.tuttle.co.jp

Second Edition
26 25 24 23
9 8 7 6 5 4

Printed in Singapore   2301MP

Asia Pacific
Berkeley Books Pte. Ltd.
3 Kallang Sector #04-01
Singapore 349278
Tel: (65) 6741 2178
Fax: (65) 6741 2179
inquiries@periplus.com.sg
www.tuttlepublishing.com

Indonesia
PT Java Books Indonesia
JI. Rawa Gelam IV No. 9
Kawasan Industri Pulogadung
Jakarta 13930
Tel: (62) 21 4682-1088
Fax: (62) 21 461-0206
cs@javabooks.co.id
www.periplus.com

TUTTLE PUBLISHING® is a registered trademark of Tuttle Publishing, a division of Periplus Editions (HK) Ltd.

For Shannon and Ian—

Because Bruce and Brandon would wish them
the richness of a happy marriage, which comes from
the artful blending of two souls

Contents

FOREWORD

The Path of an Artist

There are not a great many truly out-
standing people who pass through
our lives. These few remarkable
people leave a distinct imprint when
their chosen path in life happens
to cross ours. Indeed, an encounter
with an extraordinary human
being at a particular confluence in
the course of our daily existence may
define our destiny.

I imagine that most of us can
name only a handful of people who
have exerted such a life-changing
influence upon us. Perhaps your father or other gave you such
inspiration, a teacher or a friend, a writer or a figure from history.
Undoubtedly, because you have picked up this book, you consider
that Bruce Lee may be one of those rare individuals who has
profoundly impacted your life.

It goes without saying that my life is significantly different from
what it would have been had I not met Bruce on that momentous
day in 1963. I am grateful for the nine years of marriage that
I had the privilege of sharing with this rare and gifted individual.
In addition to the adventure of living with a thoroughly energizing
person and the joy of creating a family with him, I learned a great
deal from Bruce which has guided me through all the years since
he left.

In thinking about the enormity of the work that Bruce accomplished in his short life, I am drawn to the idea that the energy
of the soul is never extinguished with the passing of the physical
body. Even as a young man, Bruce often described "a mysterious
power" within him that motivated the paths he chose in his lifetime. I find it to be an exceptional trait that Bruce was able to
recognize and *value* the mysterious gift that burned within him. He
knew instinctively that his life had purpose, and even as he allowed

the wisdom of the ages to speak through him, he simultaneously directed his self-will toward the attainment of his visions.

Bruce often said that it is not what happens during one's life that makes the difference between people, it is the way one chooses to react to those circumstances that tests the mettle of a life well lived. Tracing the dominant patterns in Bruce's life illustrates the crucial points of choice, and, perhaps, the guidance of the mysterious power which directed his path. It was not an accident that Bruce began the study of gung fu under Master Yip Man, who instilled in him the greater meaning of martial art beyond the physical. It was not happenstance that prompted Bruce to study philosophy at the University of Washington, but the desire to infuse the spirit of philosophy into martial art. It was not by chance that, in crafting his acting skills, Bruce refused the path of the image-makers and, instead, worked to expose and express his true self. And, always, the choice of continuing self-education through voracious reading and prolific writing led Bruce down the path of expanding and broadening his potential.

Bruce was a highly educated man because he never missed an opportunity to let a "fact" or a "situation" teach him more about himself. As a scholar, he was able to turn this intellectual learning inward and make it a tool for self-cultivation. As a philosopher, he was able to apply specific principles of his art to the broader endeavor of living life as a "real" human being.

A truly extraordinary characteristic of Bruce was that he had the ability to communicate his learning process at the same time he was internalizing or living it. Whether he was teaching, acting, writing, or speaking, Bruce was able to reveal his own personal process of self-discovery. As he would have said, in his martial art and through the medium of film he was "simply and honestly expressing himself." Superficially, this could be called "charisma," but on a more profound level this ability to bare the soul should be called "artistry." Just as Michelangelo chipped away at a block of marble to reveal David, so did Bruce peel away the layers of his inner soul to expose his true self to the world.

Do you know instinctively that this is a genuine human being when you see Bruce on the screen? Is it this, then, this peeling process, that sets Bruce apart from other martial artists and actors? For those of us who knew him personally, the Bruce who was the actor is the same man we knew in real life. He was bigger than life in all ways—on and off the screen.

Bruce's words contained within this volume speak so eloquently it is hardly necessary for me to expound upon his thoughts. I simply welcome you to an opportunity to know Bruce better through sharing his insights, and perhaps then you will know yourself better, too. The ultimate destination of Bruce's journey was peace of mind— the true meaning of life. I feel confident that because Bruce chose the path of self-knowledge over accumulation of facts, and the path of self-expression over image enhancement, that he did reach his destiny with a peaceful mind. That fact gives me peace of mind. Bruce said, *"To know yourself takes a lifetime."* He did not waste a moment.

—Linda Lee Cadwell

Odyssey of an Old Soul
by Linda Lee Cadwell

The old soul wandered the length and breadth of the spiritual universe.
*The soul was wise, for it had lived in the minds of the great thinkers of the
world.*
*The soul was deep, for its wealth of human experience could fill a bottomless
lake.*
*The soul had great power, born of knowing itself through countless lives of
introspection.*
*In the realm of no-time, there are many new souls; they leave often to live
in the human world.*
*But the old soul lingered in the ethereal nothingness, awaiting the call of a
special corporeal host.*
*It happened that the heart and mind of a young boy cried out for the
attention of the old soul.*
*The immortal guest would once again grace mankind with his wisdom and
compassion.*
*For a mere thirty-two earthly years the soul burned with a passionate,
mysterious power.*
*Energizing the young man's search for truth, liberating an unparalleled
creative and spiritual force.*
*The twin captains of knowledge and wisdom were well served by the old
soul's mortal tenure, for*
*The soul of an artist dwelt among us for an imperceptible moment in the
span of time.*
*Never in vain, for, in the wake of this old soul's odyssey, a legacy of insights
was recorded*
*To enrich the heart and mind, and perhaps to age the soul, of one who dares
to gaze into the mirror of real life.*

INTRODUCTION

An *"Artist of Life"*

Approximately six months before his death, Bruce Lee wrote a profoundly personal essay, "In My Own Process," which set out his insights on the process of life. Writing from his heart, Lee jotted down his deepest feelings before they could be passed through the filter of his ego.

Over several weeks, he returned to his essay in between filming *Enter the Dragon* and drafting additional ideas for *The Game of Death.* He added more jottings as the insights came to him—at his 'office in Golden Harvest Studios, Hong Kong, in his study in Kowloon Tong, or when he went out to eat. All told, he wrote eight versions of the essay, each containing slightly more of his experiences as a martial artist, as an actor, and, most importantly, as a human being.

In the final draft of this essay (which, presumably, was written solely for Lee's own edification, as it was never published), Lee penned a rather telling statement: *"Basically, I have always been a martial artist by choice and actor by profession. But, above all, I am hoping to actualize myself to be an artist of life along the way."*[1] "Artist of life" refers to the process of being an individual who, through the use of his own independent judgment, sought to fully actualize himself as a total human being (i.e., physically, mentally, spiritually). Moreover, the "artist of life" is willing to bare his soul for the purpose of honest communication and not get caught up in societal role-playing (self-image creation). As Lee once told journalist Pierre Berton, *"It is easy for me to put on a show and be cocky and then feel pretty cool. Or I can do all kinds of phony things and be blinded by it. Or I can show you some really fancy movement. But to express oneself honestly, not lying to oneself—that, my friend, is very hard to do."*[2]

Lee sought to infuse this perspective into everything: dealing with friends, family members, and business associates; creating, choreographing, directing, and starring in films; and writing philosophical treatises, psychology papers, poetic musings, and personal essays. He told interviewer Ted Thomas: *"My life... seems to me to be a life of self-examination, a peeling of my self bit by bit, day by day."*[3] This is most evident in Lee's writing. No matter what the topic, from Chinese martial culture to heartfelt poetry, here, was a "real man" who was laying bare his soul.

Although he attended the University of Washington, the bulk of Lee's education was gained informally from his voracious reading. As he lived before the age of home computers and photocopiers, Lee wrote notes, often verbatim transcriptions in longhand, from passages he found both true and helpful. Reviewing them would inspire him to further writing. These were his private journals, where Lee contemplated the thoughts of men and women of like mind. Many of his entries (the excerpts from Eric Hoffer's *The Passionate State of Mind* and Frederick S. Perls' books on Gestalt therapy, for example) have been included, to share some of Lee's influences and the attitudes and world views he found congenial.

Ideas encountered in his reading often surfaced in his private moments. For example, in his essays on acting, he explores Perls' tenets regarding self-actualization versus self-image actualization. Finding a truth in one discipline and then applying that truth to an entirely unrelated discipline is a hallmark of Lee's genius: he saw the connections where others did not. Lee read Krishnamurti and Alan Watts on spirituality and saw a direct application to a divergent activity, martial arts. He also examined Perls' work in psychology and saw an application, not for the treatment of neuroses and depression, but for truer and more dynamic acting.

Even though these were Lee's private papers never intended for publication, they are important documents that allow us to see the evolution of Lee's beliefs and art in context. In addition to his journal entries, this volume also includes Lee's personal essays, poems, and philosophic writings on a wide range of subjects. It is therefore ironic that for over a quarter of a century Lee has been recognized primarily for his physical skills and tactical principles in the art of unarmed combat. But as *Bruce Lee, Artist of Life* reveals, such a shallow perspective is completely inaccurate.

Lee was equal parts poet, philosopher, scientist, actor, producer, director, author, choreographer, martial artist, husband, father, and friend. He sought out life in all of its wondrous aspects and was enthralled by the process of what he was experiencing. Always a thinker, Lee was fascinated by the insights into spiritual truths that could be garnered through adjusting the focus of human awareness. This is not to suggest that in reading *Artist of Life* you need to first "empty your cup" entirely of the notion of Bruce Lee the martial artist, but you do need to prepare room to meet the complete Bruce Lee, the "artist of life."

In the future, all who wish to represent themselves as torchbearers of Lee's art and philosophy will need to know ALL aspects of the man. They will as much need to know, understand, and, most importantly, *feel* the meaning underlying Lee's various drafts of the essay "In My Own Process," along with the deeper message inherent in the eight drafts of "Toward Personal Liberation (Jeet Kune Do)," for example, as they are now able to physically recite his combative techniques and repeat his martial maxims.

A great artist communicates through art. Looking at a painting, one can instantly know what the artist was feeling and thinking when he painted it. Time has no place here, as the emotion is as clear and distinct as if you were the artist yourself. Similarly, in looking at the broad and colorful strokes that Lee painted across life's canvas, we are able to intuit his personality, his passion, his heartfelt convictions, his very soul. If, as Lee once said of art, it is the "music of the soul made visible,"[4] then surely this book is his symphony.

If you read *Artist of Life* with what Lee liked to call "quiet, choiceless awareness," you will find that you are not so much reading a book as you are visiting with an old friend. And while Bruce Lee may no longer be with us physically, he is still able to communicate with us via the printed page in a manner that transcends the limits of human mortality. While appreciating his company, we should also note his counsel: become "artists of life" ourselves. We would be doing our friend and ourselves the gravest of disservices if we simply put him on a pedestal and adopted his words and beliefs as our own. In his letter (included in Part 8 of this book) to "John," Lee states as much:

You see, John,...that your way of thinking is definitely not the same as mine. Art, after all, is a means of acquiring "personal" liberty. Your way is not my way; nor mine yours. So whether or not we can get together, remember well that art "LIVES" where absolute freedom is.[5]

There is considerable danger in standing too close to the river of another's thoughts—the faster the current, the easier it is to fall in and be swept away from ourselves. Instead, let us simply enjoy watching Bruce Lee's thought as it courses through these pages, noting where it bends and turns and where it rages, froths, and bubbles with greatest energy. If we pull back and look at these thoughts from our own vantage, from where we each stand upon life's bank, we can see the bigger picture—what Lee's "finger" is pointing at. And it is at this point—where the river of one man's thoughts meets the sea of human understanding—that we will finally be able to see "all that heavenly glory" that Lee first told us about over a quarter of a century ago, and we can directly experience the awe of being fully conscious, fully human, fully alive, and fully ourselves. For, as Lee wisely observed, it is only in the process of coming to know ourselves that we can come to know anything.

—John Little

I cannot teach you; only help you to explore yourself. Nothing more.[6]

—Bruce Lee

Part 1

GUNG FU

When Bruce Lee returned to the land of his birth (America) from Hong Kong at the age of eighteen, he brought with him a vision of introducing the then little-known cultural art of Chinese gung fu to America.

Lee had at one time actually envisioned establishing chains of gung fu institutes all across America. However, as his knowledge expanded with age, and with it his philosophic and martial experiences, he no longer felt the need to extol the virtues of tradition—however venerated.

This is not to suggest that Lee ever abandoned his Chinese heritage and philosophy; he simply over time came to look for the common root of humanity, as opposed to nationality, to justify his belief system and actions. Even so, it is interesting to note that when he began to take control over the philosophy content of his films in 1972, the lessons he revealed were gleaned from the Eastern traditions.

These essays, dealing extensively with Chinese philosophy and martial art were written in the early 1960s. They are a wonderful reflection of a young Bruce Lee's driving passion to introduce and share with Westerners the beauty of his Chinese culture.

THE TAO OF GUNG FU: A STUDY IN THE WAY OF THE CHINESE MARTIAL ART

Gung fu is a special kind of skill, a fine art rather than just a physical exercise or self-defense. To the Chinese, gung fu is the subtle art of matching the essence of the mind to that of the techniques in which it has to work. The principle of gung fu is not a thing that can be learned, like a science, by fact-finding or instruction in facts. It has to grow spontaneously, like a flower, in a mind free from desires and emotions. The core of this principle of gung fu is *Tao*—the spontaneity of the universe.

The word *Tao* has no exact equivalent in the English language. To render it into the Way, or the "principle" or the "law" is to give it too narrow an interpretation. Lao-tzu, the founder of Taosim, described Tao in the following words:

> The Way that can be expressed in words is not the eternal Way; the Name that can be uttered is not the eternal Name. Conceived of as nameless it is the cause of Heaven and earth. Conceived of as having a name it is the mother of all things. Only the man eternally free from passion can contemplate its spiritual essence. He who is clogged by desires can see no more than its outer form. These two things, the spiritual (Yin) and the material (Yang), though we call them by different names, are one and the same in their origin. The sameness is a mystery of the mysteries. It is the gate of all that is subtle and wonderful.[1]

In *Masterpieces of World Philosophy:* "Tao is the nameless beginning of things, the universal principle underlying everything, the supreme, ultimate pattern, and the principle of growth."[2] Huston Smith, the author of *The World's Religions*, explained Tao as "The Way of Ultimate Reality—the Way or Principle behind all life, or the Way man should order his life to gear in with the Way the universe operates."[3]

Source: Handwritten essay by Bruce Lee entitled "The Tao of Gung Fu: A Study in the Way of the Chinese Martial Art" dated May 16, 1962. Bruce Lee Papers.

Although no one word can substitute its meaning, I have used the word *Truth* for it—the "Truth" behind gung fu; the "Truth" that every gung fu practitioner should follow.

Tao operates in Yin and Yang, a pair of mutually complementary forces that are at work in and behind all phenomena. This principle of Yin-Yang, also known as *T'ai Chi,* is the basic structure of gung fu. The T'ai Chi, or Grand Terminus, was first drawn more than three thousand years ago by Chou Chun I.

The Yang (whiteness) principle represents positiveness, firmness, masculinity, substantiality, brightness, day, heat, and so forth. The Yin (blackness) principle is the opposite. It represents negativeness, softness, femininity, insubstantiality, darkness, night, coldness, and so forth. The basic theory in T'ai Chi is that nothing is so permanent as never to change. In other words, when activity (Yang) reaches the extreme point, it becomes inactivity, and inactivity forms Yin. Extreme inactivity returns to become activity, which is Yang. Activity is the cause of inactivity and vice versa. This system of complementary increasing and decreasing of the principle is continuous. From this one can see that the two forces (Yin-Yang), although they appear to conflict, in reality are mutually interdependent; instead of opposition, there is cooperation and alternation.

The application of the principles of Yin-Yang in gung fu are expressed as the *Law of Harmony.* It states that one should be in harmony with, not in rebellion against, the strength and force of the opposition. This means that one should do nothing that is not natural or spontaneous; the important thing is not to strain in any way. When opponent A uses strength (Yang) on B, B must not resist him (back) with strength; in other words, B does not use positiveness (Yang) against positiveness (Yang), but instead yields to A with softness (Yin) and leads A in the direction of his own force, negativeness (Yin) to positiveness (Yang). When As strength goes to the extreme, the positiveness (Yang) will change to negativeness (Yin), and B can then take him at his unguarded moment and attack with force (Yang). Thus the whole process is not unnatural or strained; B fits his movement harmoniously and continuously into that of A without resisting or striving.

The above idea gives rise to a closely related law, the *Law of Noninterference with Nature,* which teaches a gung fu man to forget about himself and follow his opponent (strength) instead of himself; he does not move ahead but responds to the fitting influence. The basic idea is to defeat the opponent by yielding to him and using his own strength. That is why a gung fu man never asserts himself against his opponent, and never puts himself in frontal opposition to the direction of his opponent's force. When being attacked, he will not resist, but will control the attack by swinging with it. This law illustrates the principles of nonresistance and nonviolence, which were founded on the idea that the branches of a fir tree snap under the weight of the snow, while the simple reeds, weaker but more supple, can overcome it. In the *I'Ching,* Confucius illustrated this: "To stand in the stream is a datum of nature; one must follow and flow with it."[4] In the *Tao Te Ching,* the gospel of Taoism, Lao-tzu pointed out to us the value of gentleness. Contrary to common belief, the Yin principle, as softness and pliableness, is to be associated with life and survival. Because he can yield, a man can survive. In contrast, the Yang principle, which is assumed to be rigorous and hard, makes a man break under pressure (note the last two lines, which make a fair description of revolution as many generations of people have seen it):

> Alive, a man is supple, soft;
> In death, unbending, rigorous.
> All creatures, grass and trees, alive
> Are plastic but are pliant too,
> And dead, are friable and dry.
> Unbending rigor is the mate of death,
> And yielding softness, company of life;
> Unbending soldiers get no victories;
> The stiffest tree is readiest for the ax.
> The strong and mighty topple from their place;
> The soft and yielding rise above them all.[5]

The way of movement in gung fu is closely related to the movement of the mind. In fact, the mind is trained to direct the movement of the body. The mind wills and the body behaves. As the mind is to direct the bodily movements, the way to control the mind is important; but it is not an easy task. In his book, Glen Clark mentioned some of the emotional disturbances in athletics:

Every conflicting center, every extraneous, disrupting, decentralizing emotion, jars the natural rhythm and reduces a man's efficiency on the gridiron far more seriously than physical jars and bodily conflicts can ever jar him. The emotions that destroy the inner rhythm of a man are hatred, jealousy, lust, envy, pride, vanity, covetousness and fear.[6]

To perform the right technique in gung fu, physical loosening must be continued in a mental and spiritual loosening, so as to make the mind not only agile but free. In order to accomplish this, a gung fu man has to remain quiet and calm and to master the principle of *no-mindedness (wu-hsin)*. No-mindedness is not a blank mind that excludes all emotions; nor is it simply calmness and quietness of mind. Although quietude and calmness are important, it is the "non-graspingness" of the mind that mainly constitutes the principle of no-mindedness. A gung fu man employs his mind as a mirror—it grasps nothing and it refuses nothing; it receives but does not keep. As Alan Watts puts it, the no-mindedness is "a state of wholeness in which the mind functions freely and easily, without the sensation of a second mind or ego standing over it with a club."[7]

What he means is, let the mind think what it likes without interference by the separate thinker or ego within oneself. So long as it thinks what it wants, there is absolutely no effort in letting it go; and the disappearance of the effort to let go is precisely the disappearance of the separate thinker. There is nothing to try to do, for whatever comes up moment by moment is accepted, including nonacceptance. No-mindedness is then not being without emotion or feeling, but being one in whom feeling is not sticky or blocked. It is a mind immune to emotional influences. "Like this river, everything is flowing on ceaselessly without cessation or standing still."[8] No-mindedness is employing the whole mind as we use the eyes when we rest them upon various objects but make no special effort to take anything in. Chuang-tzu, the disciple of Lao-tzu, stated:

The baby looks at things all day without winking, that is because his eyes are not focused on any particular object. He goes without knowing where he is going, and stops without knowing what he is doing. He merges himself with the surroundings and moves along with it. These are the principles of mental hygiene.[9]

Artist of Life

Therefore, concentration in gung fu does not have the usual sense of restricting the attention to a single sense object; it is simply a quiet awareness of whatever happens to be here and now. Such concentration can be illustrated by an audience at a football game; instead of a concentrated attention on the player who has the ball, they have an awareness of the whole football field. In a similar way, a gung fu man's mind is concentrated by not dwelling on any particular part of the opponent. This is especially true when he deals with many opponents. For instance, suppose ten men are attacking him, each in succession ready to strike him down. As soon as one is disposed of, he will move on to another without permitting the mind to "stop" with any. However rapidly one blow may follow another he leaves no time to intervene between the two. Every one of the ten will thus be successively and successfully dealt with. This is possible only when the mind moves from one object to another without being "stopped" or arrested by anything. If the mind is unable to move on in this fashion, it is sure to lose the combat somewhere between two encounters.

The mind is present everywhere because it is nowhere attached

to any particular object. And it can remain present because, even when relating to this or that object, it does not cling to it. The flow of thought is like water filling a pond, which is always ready to flow off again. It can work its inexhaustible power because it is free, and it can be open to everything because it is empty. This can be compared with what Chang Chen Chi called "Serene Reflection." He wrote: "Serene means tranquility of no thought, and reflection means vivid and clear awareness. Therefore, serene reflection is clear awareness of no-thought."[10]

As stated earlier, a gung fu man aims at harmony with himself and his opponent. Also, being in harmony with one's opponent is possible not through force, which provokes conflicts and reactions, but through a yielding to the opponent's force. In other words, a gung fu man promotes the spontaneous development of his opponent and does not venture to interfere by his own action. He loses himself by giving up all subjective feelings and individuality, and he becomes one with his opponent. Inside his mind, oppositions have become mutually cooperative instead of mutually exclusive. When his private egos and conscious efforts yield to a power not his own he then achieves the supreme action, nonaction (*wu wei*).

Wu means "not" or "non" and *wei* means "action," "doing," "striving," "straining," or "busyness." Wu wei doesn't really mean doing nothing, but letting one's mind alone, trusting it to work by itself. Wu wei, in gung fu, means spontaneous action or spirit-action, in the sense that the governing force is the mind and not the senses. During sparring, a gung fu man learns to forget about himself and follow the movement of his opponent, leaving his mind free to make its own countermovement without any interfering deliberation. He frees himself from all mental suggestions of resistance and adopts a supple attitude. His actions are all performed without self-assertion; he lets his mind remain spontaneous and ungrasped. As soon as he stops to think, his flow of movement will be disturbed and his opponent will immediately strike him. Every action therefore has to be done "unintentionally" without ever "trying."

Through wu wei, a "reposeful ease" is secured. This passive achievement, as Chuang-tzu pointed out, will free a gung fu man from striving and straining himself:

A yielding will has a resposeful ease, soft as downy feathers,
A quietude, a shrinking from action, an appearance of inability
to do. Placidly free from anxiety, one acts with the opportune
time; one moves and revolves in the line of creation. One does not
move ahead but responds to the fitting influences.

Establish nothing in regard to oneself. Let things be what they
are, move like water, rest like a mirror, respond like an echo, pass
quickly like the nonexistent, and be quiet as purity. Those who
gain, lose. Do not precede others, always follow them.[11]

The natural phenomenon which the gung fu man sees as being the
closest resemblance to wu wei is water:

Nothing is weaker than water,
But when it attacks something hard
Or resistant, then nothing withstands it,
And nothing will alter its way.[12]

The above passages from the *Tao Te Ching* illustrate to us the
nature of water: Water is so fine that it is impossible to grasp a
handful of it; strike it, yet it does not suffer hurt; stab it, and it is
not wounded; sever it, yet it is not divided. It has no shape of its
own but molds itself to the receptacle that contains it. When heated
to the state of steam it is invisible but has enough power to split the
earth itself. When frozen it crystallizes into a mighty rock. First
it is turbulent like Niagara Falls, and then calm like a still pond,
fearful like a torrent, and refreshing like a spring on a hot summer's
day. So is the principle of wu wei:

The rivers and seas are lords of a hundred valleys. This is because
their strength is in lowliness; they are kings of them all. So it is that
the perfect master wishing to lead them, he follows. Thus, though
he is above them, he follows. Thus, though he is above them, men
do not feel him to be an injury. And since he will not strive, none
strive with him.[13]

The world is full of people who are determined to be somebody
or to give trouble. They want to get ahead, to stand out. Such
ambition has no use for a gung fu man, who rejects all forms
of self-assertiveness and competition:

One who tries to stand on tiptoe cannot stand still. One who stretches his legs too far cannot walk. One who advertises himself too much is ignored. One who is too insistent on his own view finds few to agree with him. One who claims too much credit does not get even what he deserves. One who is too proud is soon humiliated. These are condemned as extremes of greediness and self-destructive activity. Therefore, one who acts naturally avoids such extremes.[14]

Those who know do not speak;
Those who speak do not know.
Stop your sense
Let sharp things be blunted,
Tangles resolved,
The light tempered
And turmoil subdued;
For this is mystic unity
in which the wise man is moved
Neither by affection
Nor yet by estrangement
Or profit or loss
Or honor or shame.
Accordingly, by all the world,
He is held highest.[15]

A gung fu man, if he is really good, is not proud at all. "Pride," according to Mr. Eric Hoffer, "is a sense of worth that derives from something that is not organically part of oneself."[16] Pride emphasizes the importance of the superiority of a person's status in the eyes of others. There is fear and insecurity in pride because when a person aims at being highly esteemed and achieves such status, he is automatically involved in the fear of losing his status. Then protection of his status appears to be his most important need, and this creates anxiety. Mr. Hoffer further states that: "The less promise and potency in the self, the more imperative is the need for pride. One is proud when he identifies himself with an imaginary self; the core of pride is self-rejection."[17]

As we know, gung fu is aiming at self-cultivation, and the inner self is one's true self. So in order to realize his true self, a gung fu man lives without being dependent upon the opinion of others. Since he is completely self-sufficient he can have no fear of not being esteemed. A gung fu man devotes himself to being self-sufficient and never depends upon the external rating by others for his happiness. A gung fu master, unlike the beginner, holds himself in reserve, is quiet and unassuming, without the least desire to show off. Under the influence of gung fu training his proficiency becomes spiritual, and he himself, grown ever freer through spiritual struggle, is transformed. To him, fame and status mean nothing.

Thus wu wei is the art of artlessness, the principle of no-principle. To state it in terms of gung fu, the genuine beginner knows nothing about the way of blocking and striking, and much less about his concern for himself. When an opponent tries to strike him, he "instinctively" parries it. This is all he can do. But as soon as his training starts, he is taught how to defend and attack, where to keep the mind, and many other technical tricks—which makes his mind "stop" at various junctures. For this reason whenever he tries to strike the opponent he feels unusually hampered (he has lost altogether the original sense of innocence and freedom). But as months and years go by, as his training acquires fuller maturity, his bodily attitude and his way of managing the technique toward no-mindedness come to resemble the state of mind he had at the very beginning of training when he knew nothing, when he was altogether ignorant of the art. The beginning and the end thus turn into next-door neighbors. In the musical scale, one may start with the lowest pitch and gradually ascend to the highest. When the highest is reached, one finds it is located next to the lowest.

In a similar way, when the highest stage is reached in the study of Taoist teaching, a gung fu man turns into a kind of simpleton who knows nothing of Tao, nothing of its teachings, and is devoid of all learning. Intellectual calculations are lost sight of and a state of no-mindedness prevails. When the ultimate perfection is attained, the body and limbs perform by themselves what is assigned to them to do with no interference from the mind. The technical skill is so automatic it is completely divorced from conscious efforts.

There are big differences between the Chinese hygiene and the Western hygiene. Some of the obvious ones are Chinese exercise is rhythmic, whereas the Western is dynamic and full of tension; the Chinese exercise seeks to merge harmoniously with nature, whereas the Western dominates it; the Chinese exercise is both a way of life and a mental cultivation, while the Western exercise is merely a sport or a physical calisthenic.

Perhaps the main difference is the fact that Chinese hygiene is Yin (softness), while Western is Yang (positiveness). We can compare the Western mind with an oak tree that stands firm and rigid against the strong wind. When the wind becomes stronger, the oak tree cracks. The Chinese mind, on the other hand, is like the bamboo that bends with the strong wind. When the wind ceases (that is, when it goes to the extreme and changes), the bamboo springs back stronger than before.

Western hygiene is a gratuitous waste of energy. The overexertion and overdevelopment of bodily organs involved in Western athletics is detrimental to one's health. Chinese hygiene, on the other hand, throws its emphasis on conservation of energy; the principle is always that of moderation without going to the extreme. Whatever exercise there may be consists of harmonious movements calculated to normalize but not to excite one's bodily regimen. It starts out with a mental regimen as a basis, in which the sole object is to bring about peace and calmness of mind. With this as a basis, it aims at stimulating the normal functioning of the internal process of respiration and blood circulation.

GUNG FU: THE CENTER OF THE ORIENTAL ARTS

Gung fu, the center of the Oriental arts of self-defense, is a philosophical art that serves to promote health, to cultivate the mind, and to provide a most efficient means of self-protection.

Its philosophy is based on the integral parts of the philosophies of Taoism and Chan (Zen)—the ideal of being harmonious with and not against the force of the opponent. Just as a butcher preserves his knife by cutting along the bones, a gung fu man preserves himself by complementing the movements of the opponent.

The word gung fu means "discipline" and "training" toward the ultimate reality of the object—be it health promotion, mind cultivation or self-protection. There is no distinction to make between the opponent and the self because the opponent is but the other complementary (not opposite) part. There is no conquering, struggling, or dominating, and the idea is to "fit" harmoniously your movement into that of the opponent. When he expands, you contract; when he contracts, you expand. Expansion then is interdependent with contraction and vice versa, each being the cause and result of the other.

Source: Bruce Lee's handwritten essay on gung fu, untitled. Bruce Lee Papers.

Gentleness/firmness is one inseparable force of one unceasing interplay of movement. If a person riding a bicycle wishes to go somewhere, he cannot pump on both the pedals at the same time or not pump on them at all. In order to move forward he has to pump on one pedal and release the other. So the movement of going forward requires this "oneness" of pumping and releasing. Therefore, gentleness alone cannot forever dissolve away great force, nor can sheer brute force subdue one's foe. In order to survive in any combat, the harmonious interfusion of gentleness and firmness as a whole is necessary, sometimes one dominating sometimes the other, in a wavelike succession. The movement will then truly flow, for the pure fluidity of movements is in their interchangeability.

So neither gentleness nor firmness holds any more than one half of a broken whole which, welded together, forms the true Way of martial art. The tendency to guard against is from getting too firm and stiff. Notice that the stiffest tree is most easily cracked, while the bamboo or willow survives by bending with the wind. This is why a gung fu man is soft yet not yielding, firm, yet not hard. The best example of gung fu is water. Water can penetrate the hardest granite because it is yielding. One cannot stab or strike at water and hurt it because that which offers no resistance cannot be overcome.

In actual application, gung fu is based on simplicity; it is a natural result of four thousand years of exhaustive experimentation and is of highly sophisticated complexity. All techniques are stripped down to their essential purpose without wastage or ornamentation, and everything becomes the straightest, most logical simplicity of common sense. The utmost is expressed and performed in the minimum of movements and energy.

The method for health promotion is again based on water, as flowing water never grows stale. The idea is not to overdevelop or to overexert but to normalize the function of the body.

Bruce Lee (right) and his only formal martial art instructor, Yip Man.

I-C

A MOMENT OF UNDERSTANDING

Gung fu is a special kind of skill, a fine art rather than just a physical exercise. It is a subtle art of matching the essence of the mind to that of the techniques in which it has to work. The principle of gung fu is not a thing

The principle of gung fu is not a thing that can be learned, like a science, by fact-finding and instruction in facts. It has to grow spontaneously, like a flower, in a mind free from emotions and desires.

that can be learned, like a science, by fact-finding and instruction in facts. It has to grow spontaneously, like a flower, in a mind free from emotions and desires. The core of this principle of gung fu is Tao—the spontaneity of the universe.

Source: Bruce Lee's handwritten essay entitled "A Moment of Understanding" from one of his courses at the University of Washington. Bruce Lee Papers. Subsequently published on pages 134-36 in Volume 2 of The Bruce Lee Library Series entitled The Tao of Gung Fu: A Study in the Way of Chinese Martial Art, written by Bruce Lee, edited by John Little, published by the Charles E. Tuttle Publishing Company, Boston, (c) 1997 Linda Lee Cadwell.

After four years of hard training in the art of gung fu, I began to understand and felt the principle of gentleness—the art of neutralizing the effect of the opponent's effort and minimizing the expenditure of one's energy.

All these must be done in calmness and without striving. It sounded simple, but in actual application it was difficult.

The moment I engaged in combat with an opponent, my mind was completely perturbed and unstable. And after a series of exchanging blows and kicks, my theory of gentleness was gone. My only thought at this point was "Somehow or other I must beat him and win!"

My instructor at the time, Professor Yip Man, head of the wing chun school of gung fu, would come up to me and say "Loong,[18] relax and calm your mind. Forget about yourself and follow the opponent's movement. Let your mind, the basic reality, do the counter-movement without any interfering deliberation. Above all, learn the art of detachment."

"That was it!" I thought. "I must relax!" However, right then I had just done something that contradicted against my will. That occurred at the precise moment I said, "I must relax." The demand for effort in *must* was already inconsistent with the effortlessness in *relax*.

The moment I engaged in combat with an opponent, my mind was completely perturbed and unstable. And after a series of exchanging blows and kicks, my theory of gentleness was gone. My only thought at this point was "Somehow or other I must beat him and win!"

When my acute self-consciousness grew to what the psychologists refer to as the "double-bind" type, my instructor would again approach me and say, "Loong, preserve you by following the natural bends of things and don't interfere. Remember never to assert yourself against nature; never be in frontal opposition to any problems, but control it by swinging with it. Don't practice this week. Go home and think about it."

The following week I stayed home. After spending many hours meditating and practicing, I gave up and went sailing alone in a junk. On the sea I thought of all my past training and got mad at myself and punched the water! Right then—at that moment—a thought suddenly struck me; was not this water the very essence of gung fu? Hadn't this water just now illustrated to me the principle of gung fu? I struck it but it did not suffer hurt. Again I struck it with all of my might—yet it was not wounded! I then tried to grasp a handful of it but this proved impossible. This water, the softest substance in the world, which could be contained in the smallest jar, only seemed weak. In reality, it could penetrate the hardest substance in the world. That was it! I wanted to be like the nature of water.

Suddenly a bird flew by and cast its reflection on the water. Right then as I was absorbing myself with the lesson of the water, another mystic sense of hidden meaning revealed itself to me; should not the thoughts and emotions I had when in front of an opponent pass like the reflection of the bird flying over the water? This was exactly what Professor Yip meant by being detached—not being without emotion or feeling, but being one in whom feeling was not sticky or blocked. Therefore in order to control myself I must first accept myself by going with and not against my nature

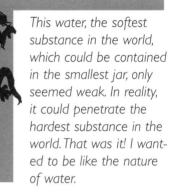

This water, the softest substance in the world, which could be contained in the smallest jar, only seemed weak. In reality, it could penetrate the hardest substance in the world. That was it! I wanted to be like the nature of water.

I lie on the boat and felt that I had united with Tao; I had become one with nature. I just lay there and let the boat drift freely according to its own will. For at that moment I had achieved a state of inner feeling in which opposition had become mutually cooperative instead of mutually exclusive, in which there was no longer any conflict in my mind. The whole world to me was unitary.

REFLECTIONS ON GUNG FU

Gung fu is so extraordinary because it is nothing at all special. It is simply the direct expression of one's feeling with the minimum of lines and energy. Every movement is being so of itself without the artificiality with which we tend to complicate them. The closer to the true Way of gung fu, the less wastage of expression there is.

Gung fu is to be looked at without fancy suits and matching ties, and it remains a secret while we anxiously look for sophistication and deadly techniques. If there are really any secrets at all, they must have been missed by the "seeing" and "striving" of its practitioners (after all, how many ways are there to come in on an opponent without deviating too much from the natural course?). Gung fu values the wonder of the ordinary, and the idea is not daily increase but daily decrease.

Source: An article written by Bruce Lee that was never published, written on December 21, 1964, to illustrate the different techniques used by the different schools of gung fu. Bruce Lee Papers.

Artist of Life

Being wise in gung fu does not mean adding more but being able to remove sophistication and ornamentation and be simply simple—like a sculptor building a statue not by adding, but by hacking away the unessential so that the truth will be revealed unobstructed. Gung fu is satisfied with one's bare hands without the fancy decoration of colorful gloves, which tend to hinder the natural function of the hands. The height of cultivation always runs to simplicity while halfway cultivation runs to ornamentation.

There are three stages in the cultivation of gung fu: namely, the primitive stage, the stage of art, and the stage of artlessness. The primitive stage is the stage of original ignorance in which a person knows nothing of the art of combat. In a fight he "simply" blocks and strikes instinctively without concern as for what is right and wrong. Of course, he might not be so-called scientific, but he is, nevertheless, being himself.

The second stage, *the stage of art*, begins when a person starts his training. He is taught the different ways of blocking and striking, the various ways of kicking, of standing, of moving, of breathing, of thinking. Unquestionably he is gaining a scientific knowledge of combat, but unfortunately his original self and sense of freedom are lost, and his action no longer flows by itself. His mind tends to freeze at different movements for calculation and analysis. Even worse, he might be "intellectually bound" and maintaining himself outside the actual reality.

The third stage, *the stage of artlessness*, occurs when, after years of serious and hard practice, he realizes that, after all, gung fu is nothing special and instead of trying to impose his mind on the art, he adjusts himself to the opponent like water pressing on an earthen wall—it flows through the slightest crack. There is nothing to "try" to do but be purposeless and formless like water. Nothingness prevails; he no longer is confined.

These three stages also apply to the various methods being practiced in Chinese gung fu. Some methods are rather primitive with basic jerky blocking and striking. On the whole, they lack the flow and change of combinations. Some "sophisticated" methods, on the other hand, tend to run to ornamentation and get carried away by grace and showmanship. Whether from the so-called "firm" or "gentle" school, they often involve big, fancy movements with a lot of complicated steps toward one single goal (it is like an artist who, not satisfied with drawing a simple snake, proceeds to put four beautiful and shapely feet on the snake).

When grasped by the collar, for example, these practitioners would "first do this, then this, and finally that"—but of course the direct way would be to let the opponent have the pleasure of grasping the collar (he is grasping it anyway) and simply punch him straight on the nose! To some martial artists of distinguishing taste, this would be a little bit unsophisticated; too ordinary and unartful. However, it is the ordinary that we use and encounter in everyday life.

Art is the expression of the self; the more complicated and restrictive a method is, the less opportunity there is for expression of one's original sense of freedom. The techniques, although they play an important role in the earlier stage, should not be too complex, restrictive, or mechanical. If we cling to them we will become bound by their limitations.

Remember that man created method, and method did not create man, and do not strain yourself in twisting into someone's preconceived pattern, which unquestionably would be appropriate for him, but not necessarily for you. You yourself are "expressing" the technique and not "doing" the technique; in fact, there is no doer but the action itself. When someone attacks you, it is not technique number one (or is it "technique number two?") that you use, but the moment you're aware of his attack you simply move in like sound, an echo without any deliberation. It is as though when I call, you answer me, or when I throw something, you catch it. That's all.

After all these years of practice in the different schools I have found out this: that techniques are merely simple guide lines to tell the practitioner that he has done enough! Of course, different people have different preferences and therefore I will include different techniques of both the Northern and the Southern schools of gung fu. Observe closely the differences as well as the similarities of utilization.

TEACH YOURSELF SELF-DEFENSE

What would you do if you were attacked by a thug? Would you stand your ground and fight it out? Or, if you will excuse me, would you say that you would run like hell? But what if your loved ones were with you? What then? That's the all-important question.

You have only to pick up a newspaper to read of attacks made, not only on lonely commons, but also in built-up areas, to understand the need for self-defense. "To be forewarned is to be forearmed" is an old, reliable proverb, and the purpose of my notes on self-defense is not only to forewarn you, but to forearm you with practical knowledge about meeting any foe, regardless of his size and strength.

Some Tips on Self-Defense

Self-defense is not fun. You are liable to find yourself fighting hard to avoid serious injury and so you must expect to be hurt. The method of self-defense I am going to describe will not prevent your being hurt, but it will give you a very good chance of emerging the victor without sustaining any severe injury. You will have to accept this, and should a blow from your opponent break through, it is essential—at least for the time being—to ignore the pain and, instead of giving up, use [it] as a spur to counterattack and victory. (Bear this in mind: when being attacked by a thug the fact is that he has but a one-track mind, which is bent on your destruction, rarely considering what you can do. If your acts show him that he is up against something he did not expect, it will cut down his attacking ego over 50 percent and will neutralize his attack, in which case you always have the psychological advantage on your side.)

Source: Bruce Lee's handwritten essay entitled "Teach Yourself Self-Defense," dated 1962. Bruce Lee Papers.

This may not sound very encouraging, but the chances of attack can be very greatly reduced when you are walking, especially alone at night or in lonely places, if you are always alert. Keep an eye on any person who appears to be following you or who approaches. Keep to the outside of the path or in the middle of a lane. Listen for approaching footsteps and watch shadows; that is to say, as you pass a street lamp you will see the shadow of anyone behind you thrown up on the ground in front of you. The same thing happens as the result of lights in houses and the headlights of passing cars. As soon as you see a shadow in these circumstances, immediately glance around and see who it is. Always, of course, avoid patches of deep shadow.

In made-up but quiet streets, I repeat, walk on the outside of the pavement. This obviates the chance of anyone jumping out of a house or garden entrance at you to snatch your purse, handbag, or briefcase or worse. For exactly the same reason I

The main thing is to see the attack coming, which enables you to shout, scream, or just concentrate on dealing with the attacker. Make as much noise as possible as this naturally tends to frighten off lawbreakers.

suggest walking down the middle of a lane where there are no made-up paths and perhaps no street lamps. If you consider it advisable, you may even cross the road to avoid a person of whom you are suspicious. If he follows, he at least makes his intention fairly obvious. Although I am again repeating myself, I must emphasize that the success of an [assailant's] attack depends on surprise, and if you're sufficiently alert to prevent a surprise, your counterattack is already halfway to being successful. The main thing is to see the attack coming, which enables you to shout, scream, or just concentrate on dealing with the attacker. Make as much noise as possible as this naturally tends to frighten off lawbreakers.

I hope I have not frightened you and made you think it is not safe to walk along the streets. That is certainly not my intention, but newspaper reports lead one to believe that attacks on innocent people are increasing.

The Basis of Self-Defense

There is only one basic principle of self-defense: You must apply the most effective weapon as soon as possible to the most vulnerable point of your enemy. Although I say there is only one basic principle, it is better to break it into sections and look at it more thoroughly:

1. what is the most effective weapon
2. speed
3. the point to attack or counterattack

The Weapon

Given a choice I would always choose the leg. It is longer than the arm and can deal a heavier blow, and it is much more powerful. So, should anyone approach you, your kick would make contact before his punch, if both commence at the same speed.

Speed

There is no time to consider the type of defense or weapon to use. Obviously, if your kick does not commence, his punch will land first, and your defense is useless. Only training can produce results (I can help you with this). If you do not consider a few minutes' training worth-while, and you think the chance of assault is small, you are one of those people who encourage thugs to attack, and no one can help you should an emergency arise.

There is only one basic principle of self-defense: You must apply the most effective weapon as soon as possible to the most vulnerable point of your enemy.

The Point of Counterattack

Among the most vulnerable points for your counter if you are attacked by a man are the groin, eyes, abdomen, and knee.

PSYCHOLOGY IN DEFENSE AND ATTACK

Size is never a true indication of muscular power and efficiency. The smaller man usually makes up for the imbalance of power by his greater agility, flexibility, speed of foot, and nervous action.

Bear this in mind once you go into action and grapple with an opponent: strive to keep him off balance, regardless of his size. So keep moving faster than he and pay absolutely no attention to his size, fierce facial contortions, or his vicious language. Your object is always to attack your opponent at his weakest points, which are mainly gravitational, throwing him off balance, and applying leverage principles so that his body, and the limbs of his body, are used to work toward his own defeat. "The bigger they are, the harder they fall."

In combating a man with your bare hands, you must learn to use your head, knees, and feet as well as your hands. The "crowding" act gives you every opportunity to use these

In combating a man with your bare hands, you must learn to use your head, knees, and feet as well as your hands. The "crowding" act gives you every opportunity to use these parts of your body, especially your elbows.

parts of your body, especially your elbows. Another simple method while crowding with your opponent is to step on your opponent's foot. It has unexpected results. The one point to bear in mind when you are being attacked by a thug is the fact that the thug has but a one-track mind. He thinks in but one groove, which is bent on your destruction, rarely considering what you can do, in which case you always have the psychological advantage on your side. With efficiency comes confidence and self-reliance.

Source: Bruce Lee's handwritten essay from his pocket journal, entitled "Psychology in Defense and Attack," circa 1961.

Artist of Life

HOW TO CHOOSE A MARTIAL ART INSTRUCTOR

I sincerely give this advice to all readers who are about to take up martial art: believe only half of what you see and definitely nothing that you hear.

Before you take any lessons from any instructor, find out clearly from him what his method is and politely request that he demonstrate to you how some techniques operate. Use your common sense, and if he convinces you, then by all means go ahead.

How does one judge if an instructor is good? Rather, this question should be rephrased to read How can one judge if a method or system is good? After all, one cannot learn the speed or power of an instructor, but one can assess his skill. Thus the soundness of the system, and not the instructor, is to be considered; the instructor is merely there to point the way and lead his disciples to an awareness that he himself is the one and only one to give true feeling and expression to the system.

The system should not be mechanical and complicated, but simply simple, with no "magical power." The method (which is ultimately no method) is there to remind one when he has done enough. The techniques have no magical power and are nothing special; they are merely the simplicity of profound common sense.

Do not, however, be impressed by instructors who have brick-breaking hands, invincible stomachs, iron forearms, or even speed, for that matter. Remember, you cannot learn his ability, but you can learn his skill. At any rate, the ability to break stones, to take a punch on the body, to jump so many feet off the ground are but stunts in the Chinese art of gung fu. Of primary importance are the techniques.

Source: An essay from Bruce Lee's handwritten manuscript for the book The Tao of Gung Fu, originally drafted in 1964 and reprinted in Volume 2 of The Bruce Lee Library Series entitled The Tao of Gung Fu: A Study in the Way of Chinese Martial Art, written by Bruce Lee, edited by John Little, published by the Charles E. Tuttle Publishing Company, Boston, (c) 1997 Linda Lee Cadwell.

Breaking a brick and punching a human being are two different things: a brick does not give, whereas when being hit, a human being spins, falls, and so forth, thus dissolving the power of the blow. What is the use if one has no technique to bring home his so-called "killing stroke"? On top of that, bricks and stones do not move and fight back. Thus, the system should be the thing considered, and, as mentioned before, a system should not be mechanical, intricate, and fanciful, but simply simple.

What if the "master" does not wish to show you his style? What if he is "too humble" and firmly guards his "deadly" secret? One thing I hope readers should realize regarding Oriental humility and secrecy is that although it is true that highly qualified teachers do not boast and sometimes do not teach gung fu to just anybody, the fact remains that they are only human beings, and certainly they have not spent ten, twenty, or thirty years on an art in order to say nothing about it. Even Lao-tzu, the author of the *Tao Teh Ching,* and the man who wrote "He who knows does not speak. He who speaks, does not know," wrote five-thousand words to explain his doctrine.

In order to be able to pass for being more than their ability, the honorable masters, professors, and experts (in America, especially) say little. They certainly have mastered the Oriental highest way of humility and secrecy, for it is definitely easier to look wise than to talk wisely (to act wisely is, of course, even more difficult). The more one wants to pass at a value above his worth, the more he will keep his mouth shut. For once he talks (or moves), people can certainly classify him accordingly.

The unknown is always wonderful and the "fifteenth-degree red belt holders," the "experts from super advanced schools," and the "honorable masters" know how to gather around them a mysterious veil of secrecy. There is a Chinese saying that applies to these people: "Silence is the ornament and safeguard of the ignorant."

THE UNITY OF GENTLENESS/FIRMNESS

Many times I have heard instructors from different schools claim that their systems of gentleness require absolutely no strength (strength has become an ugly word to them), and that with merely a flick of one's little finger, one can send his 306½-pound helpless opponent flying through the air.

We must face the fact that strength, though used in a much more refined way, is necessary in combat, and that an average opponent doesn't charge blindly with his head down (not even a football tackier will do that). Some instructors, on the other hand, claim that with their super powerful system, one can smash through any defense. Once again we must realize that a person does move and change just as a reed of bamboo moves back and forth in a storm to "dissolve" the strong wind.

So neither gentleness nor firmness holds any more than half of a broken whole, which, fitted together, forms the true Way of gung fu. Gentleness/firmness is one inseparable force of one unceasing interplay of movement. They are conceived of as essentially one, or as two coexistent forces of one indivisible whole.

So neither gentleness nor firmness holds any more than half of a broken whole, which fitted together, forms the true Way of gung fu. Gentleness/firmness is one inseparable force of one unceasing interplay of movement. They are conceived of as essentially one, or as two coexistent forces of one indivisible whole.

If a person riding a bicycle wishes to go somewhere, he cannot pump on both pedals at the same time or not pump on them at all. In order to go somewhere he has to pump on one pedal and release

Source: Bruce Lee's handwritten notes entitled "*The Tao of 'Jeet Kune.*' The Way of the '*Stopping Fist,*' Chinese Boxing from the Jun Fan Gung Fu Institute," circa 1967, Bruce Lee Papers.

the other. So the movement of going forward requires this "oneness" of pumping and releasing. Pumping is the result of releasing and vice versa, each being the cause and result of the other. The movement will then truly flow, for the true fluidity of movement is in its interchangeability.

Any practitioner of martial art should consider both the gentleness and the firmness of equal importance, and not as being independent of one another. The rejection of either gentleness or firmness will lead to separation, and separation runs to extremes.

Any practitioner of martial art should consider both the gentleness and the firmness of equal importance, and not as being independent of one another. The rejection of either gentleness or firmness will lead to separation, and separation runs to extremes.

Gentleness and firmness are not isolated but are complementary as well as contrastive, and in their interfusion they make up the "oneness." Always remember this fact, and if you do not favor so much on the side of either firmness or gentleness, you can then truly appreciate the "good/bad" of them. Gentleness versus firmness is not the situation, but gentleness/firmness as a oneness is the true Way.

Artist of Life

MY VIEW ON GUNG FU

Some instructors of martial art favor forms, the more complex and fancy the better. Some, on the other hand, are obsessed with super-mental power (like Captain Marvel or Superman). Still some favor deformed hands and legs and devote their time to fighting bricks, stones, boards, and so forth, and so on.

To me the extraordinary aspect of gung fu lies in its simplicity. Gung fu is simply the "direct expression" of one's feeling with the minimum of movements and energy. Every movement is being so of itself without the artificialities with which people tend to complicate it. The easy way is always the right way, and gung fu is nothing at all special; the closer to the true Way of gung fu, the less wastage of expression there is.

Instead of facing combat in its suchness, quite a few systems of martial art accumulate a "fancy mess" that distorts and cramps their practitioners and distracts them from the actual reality of combat, which is "simple" and "direct" and "nonclassical." Instead of going immediately to the heart of things, flowery forms and artificial techniques (organized despair!) are "ritually practiced" to simulate actual combat. Thus instead of "being" in combat, these practitioners are idealistically "doing" something about combat. Worse still, supermental this and spiritual that are ignorantly incorporated until these practitioners are drifting further and further into the distance of abstraction and mystery, until what they do resembles anything from acrobatics to modern dancing, but not the actual reality of combat.

All these complex messes are actually futile attempts to "arrest" and "fix" the ever-changing movements in combat and to dissect and analyze them like a corpse. Real combat is not fixed and is very much "alive." Such means of practice (a form of paralysis) will only "solidify" and "condition" what was once fluid and alive.

Source: A typed essay of Bruce Lee's entitled "My View on Gung Fu" that Bruce Lee handed out to members of the Oakland and Los Angeles chapters of his Jun Fan Gung Fu Institutes, circa 1967.

When you get off sophistication and whatnot and look at it "realistically," these robots (practitioners, that is) are blindly devoting themselves to the systematic uselessness of practicing "routines" or "stunts" that lead nowhere.

Gung fu is to be looked through without fancy suits and matching ties, and it will remain a secret when we anxiously look for sophistication and deadly techniques. If there are really any secrets at all, they must have been missed by the seeking and striving of its practitioners (after all, how many ways are there to come in on an opponent without "deviating too much from the natural course"?). True, gung fu values the wonder of the ordinary, and the cultivation of gung fu is not daily increase but daily decrease. Being wise in gung fu does not mean adding more, but to be able to do away with ornamentation and be simply simple—like a sculptor building a statue not by adding, but by hacking away the unessential so that the truth will be revealed unobstructed. In short, gung fu is satisfied with one's bare hands without the fancy decoration of colorful gloves, which tend to hinder the natural function of the hand.

Art is the expression of the self. The more complicated and restrictive a method is, the less the opportunity there will be for the expression of one's original sense of freedom! The techniques, though they play an important role in the early stage, should not be too restrictive, complex, or mechanical. If we cling to them we will become bound by their limitations. Remember, *you* are "expressing" the technique and not "doing" the technique. When someone attacks you it is not technique number one (or is it technique number two, stance two, section four?) that you are doing, but the moment you are "aware" of his attack you simply move in like sound and echo without deliberation. It is as though when I call you, you answer me, or when I throw something to you, you catch it. That's all.

Part 2

PHILOSOPHY

It may surprise those who think of Bruce Lee primarily as a martial artist that his true passion was philosophy. Even more surprising is the extent of his knowledge of both Eastern and Western philosophy.

These essays were largely composed during the years that Lee attended the University of Washington, where he majored in philosophy. This period of his life contributed immensely to broadening his intellect and his exposure to Western theoretical thought. He read Plato, David Hume, Rene Descartes, Thomas Aquinas (a church father whom Lee had also probably absorbed through osmosis during his Catholic school upbringing in Hong Kong during the 1950s).

Moreover, these essays reveal Lee's thought processes with regard to his worldview or metaphysics. His earlier research and beliefs regarding Taoism, for example, particularly its metaphysic of monism, are not only left intact after being subjected to the barrage of the best of Western theoretical thought, but in fact they are strengthened by the exposure.

Of even more interest, however, is the fact that these essays reveal themes that Lee would come to understand and express even more succinctly as he grew older, serving to sow the seeds of independent inquiry and the need for rational justification. They remain among his most eloquent and thought-provoking writings.

2-A

WHY I TOOK TO PHILOSOPHY

When I returned from Thailand with the work crew of Golden Harvest Ltd. after the completion of *The Big Boss,* many people started asking me this: What was it that made me give up my career in the States and return to Hong Kong to shoot Chinese films?

Perhaps the general feeling was that it was all hell to have to work on Chinese films since the Chinese film industry was still so underdeveloped. To the above question I find no easy explanation except that I am Chinese and I have to

My old man was a famous artist of the Chinese opera and was popularly accepted by the people. Hence he spent a lot of time performing in the States. I was born when he brought my mother along during one of his performance trips.

fulfill my duty as a Chinese. The truth is, I am an American-born Chinese. That I should become an American-born Chinese was accidental, or it might have been my father's arrangement. At that time, the Chinese inhabitants in the States, mostly from the province of Kwangtung, were very much homesick: nostalgia was held towards everything that was associated with their homeland.

In this context, Chinese opera, with its unmistakably unique Chinese characteristics, won the day. My old man was a famous artist of the Chinese opera and was popularly accepted by the people. Hence he spent a lot of time performing in the States. I was born when he brought my mother along during one of his performance trips.

Yet my father did not want me to receive an American education. When I reached my school age, he sent me back to Hong Kong—his second homeland—to live with his kinsmen. It could have been a matter of heredity or environment; I came to be greatly interested

Source: A Taiwan newspaper article written by Bruce Lee, entitled "Me and Jeet Kune Do," dated 1972, reprinted in the magazine *Bruce Lee: Studies On Jeet Kune Do,* (c) 1976, Bruce Lee Jeet Kune Do Club, Hong Kong, and reprinted in its entirety in Volume I of the Bruce Lee Library Series *Words of the Dragon.*

in the making of films when I was studying in Hong Kong. My father was then well acquainted with lots of movie stars and directors. Among whom there was the late Mr. Chin Kam. They brought me into the studio and gave me some roles to play. I started off as a bit player and gradually became the star of the show.

That was a very crucial experience in my life. For the first time I was confronted with genuine Chinese culture. The sense of being part of it was so strongly felt that I was enchanted. I didn't realize it then, nor did I see how great an influence environment can have on the molding of one's character

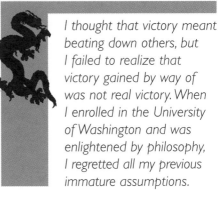

I thought that victory meant beating down others, but I failed to realize that victory gained by way of was not real victory. When I enrolled in the University of Washington and was enlightened by philosophy, I regretted all my previous immature assumptions.

and personality. Nevertheless, the notion of "being Chinese" was then duly conceived.

From boyhood to adolescence, I presented myself as a trouble-maker and was greatly disapproved of by my elders. I was extremely mischievous, aggressive, hot-tempered, and fierce. Not only my "opponents" of more or less my age stayed out of my way, but even the adults sometimes gave in to my temper. I never knew what it was that made me so pugnacious. The first thought that came into my mind whenever I met somebody I disliked was, "Challenge him!" Challenge him with what? The only concrete thing that I could think of was my fists. I thought that victory meant beating down others, but I failed to realize that victory gained by way of force was not real victory. When I enrolled in the University of Washington and was enlightened by philosophy, I regretted all my previous immature assumptions.

My majoring in philosophy was closely related to the pugnacity of my childhood. I often ask myself these questions:
- What comes after victory?
- Why do people value victory so much?
- What is "glory"?
- What kind of "victory" is "glorious"?

Artist of Life

When my tutor assisted me in choosing my courses, he advised me to take up philosophy because of my inquisitiveness. He said, "Philosophy will tell you what man lives for." When I told my friends and relatives that I had picked up philosophy, they were all amazed. Everybody thought I had better go into physical education since the only extra-curricular activity that I was interested in, from my childhood until I graduated from my secondary school, was Chinese martial arts. As a matter of fact, martial arts and philosophy seem to be antithetical to each other. But I think that the theoretical part of Chinese martial arts seems to be getting indistinct.

Every action should have its why and wherefore; and there ought to be a complete and proficient theory to back up the whole concept of Chinese martial arts. I wish to infuse the spirit of philosophy into martial arts; therefore I insisted on studying philosophy.

I have never discontinued studying and practicing martial arts. While I am tracing the source and history of Chinese martial arts, this doubt always comes up: Now that every branch of Chinese gung fu has its own form, its own established style, are these the original intentions of their founders? I don't think so. Formality could be a hindrance to progress; this is applicable to everything, including philosophy. Philosophy brings my jeet kune do into a new realm in the sphere of martial arts, and jeet kune do brings my acting career to a new horizon.

REGARDING HUMAN UNDERSTANDING

With regard to human understanding there are simple impressions and simple ideas. A simple impression has a stronger and more vivid picture than a simple idea and is also the cause of a simple idea.

In other words, simple ideas are copies of the simple impressions. For example, I see something exciting, and that certain something moves me, and because of this impression I can later on have an idea of it. Therefore simple ideas are direct copies of simple impressions and cannot be broken into parts but are a unified whole.

Although complex impressions and complex ideas are in general a copy of the other (complex ideas are copies of complex impressions), in some unusual cases they are not so. For instance, I can imagine a place where I have never been, or in the case of a man who is color blind of the color blue, he may make up his own idea of that color based on his experience of the other colors.

The term "complex idea," by the way, signifies something that is constituted of simple ideas. For instance, an apple that has color, taste, size, and so forth.

Source: Bruce Lee's handwritten philosophy paper from the University of Washington, February 18, 1964. Bruce Lee Papers.

Artist of Life

2-C

LIVING: THE ONENESS OF THINGS

Many philosophers are among those who say one thing and do another, and the philosophy that a man professes is often quite other than the one he lives by. Philosophy is in danger of becoming more and more only something professed.

Philosophy is not "living" but an activity concerning theoretic knowledge, and most philosophers are not going to live things, but simply to theorize about them, to contemplate them. And to contemplate a thing implies maintaining oneself outside it, resolved to keep a distance between it and ourselves.

In life, we accept naturally the full reality of what we see and feel in general with no shadow of a doubt. Philosophy, however, does not accept what life believes; it strives to convert reality into a problem. Like asking such questions as "Is this chair that I see in front of me really there?" "Can it exist by itself?" Thus, rather than making life easy for living by living in accord with life, philosophy complicates it by replacing the world's tranquility with the restlessness of problems. It is like asking a normal person how he actually breathes! That will immediately choke the breath out of him when he consciously describes the process. Why try to arrest and interrupt the flow of life? Why create such fuss? A person simply breathes.

Source: Bruce Lee's handwritten essay entitled "Living: The 'Oneness' of Things," circa 1963. Bruce Lee Papers.

The Western approach to reality is mostly through theory, and theory begins by denying reality—to talk about reality, to go around reality, to catch anything that attracts our senses—intellect and abstract it away from reality itself. Thus philosophy begins by saying that the outside world is not a basic fact, that its existence can be doubted, and that every proposition in which the reality of the outside world is affirmed is not an evident proposition but one that needs to be divided, dissected, and analyzed. It is to stand consciously aside and try to square a circle.

Rene Descartes (1596-1650), the great French philosopher and mathematician, raised the above problem. Since existence of anything, including my being, is not certain, what is there in the universe beyond any shadow of a doubt? When one has doubts about the world, and even about the whole entire universe what is left? Let's "stand" outside this world for a moment and follow Descartes and see what is actually left.

According to Descartes, the doubt itself is left, because for something to be doubtful, it must seem to me that it is; and the whole universe may seem to me doubtful, except for the fact of its seeming to me. To doubt is to think, and thought is the only thing in the universe whose existence cannot be denied, because to deny is to think. When one says that thought exists, it automatically includes saying that one exists because there is no thought that does not contain as one of its elements a subject who thinks.

In Chinese Taoism and Ch'an (Zen) the world is seen as an inseparable, interrelated field, no part of which can actually be separated from the other. That is, there would be no bright stars without dim stars, and, without the surrounding darkness, no stars at all. Oppositions have become mutually dependent instead of mutually exclusive, and there is no longer any conflict between the individual man and nature.

So if thought exists, I who think and the world about which I think also exist; the one exists but for the other, there being no possible separation between them. Therefore, the world and I are both in active correlation; I am that which sees the world, and the world is that which is seen by me. I exist for the world, and the world exists for me. If there were no things to be seen, thought about, and imagined, I would not see, think, or imagine. That is to

Artist of Life

say, I would not exist. One sure and primary and fundamental fact is the joint existence of a subject and its world. The one does not exist without the other. I acquire no understanding of myself except as I take account of objects, of the surroundings. I do not think unless I think of things—and therefore, find myself.

It is of no use to talk merely about objects of consciousness, whether they are thought sensations or wax candles. An object must have a subject, and subject-object is a pair of complementaries (not opposites), like all others, which are two halves of one whole, and are a function each of the other. When we hold to the core, the opposite sides are the same if they are seen from the center of the moving circle. I do not experience; I am experience. I am not the subject of an experience; I am that experience. I am awareness. Nothing else can be I or can exist.

Thus we do not sweat because it is hot; the sweating is the heat. It is just as true to say that the sun is light because of the sun. This peculiar Chinese viewpoint is unfamiliar because it is our settled convention to think that heat comes first and then, by causality, the body sweats. To put it the other way round is startling, like saying "cheese and bread" instead of "bread and cheese." This shocking and seemingly illogical reversal of common sense may perhaps be clarified by the following illustration of "the moon in the water."

The Moon in the Water

The phenomenon of the moon in the water is likened to human experience. The water is the subject, and the moon the object. When there is no water, there is no moon in the water, and likewise when there is no moon. But when the moon rises, the water does not wait to receive its image, and when even the tiniest drop of water is poured out, the moon does not wait to cast its reflection. For the moon does not intend to cast its reflection, and the water does not receive the moon's image on purpose. The event is caused as much by the water as by the moon, and as the water manifests the brightness of the moon, the moon manifests the clarity of the water.

Everything does have a real relationship, a mutuality in which the subject creates the object just as much as the object creates the subject. Thus the knower no longer feels himself to be separated from the known; the experiencer no longer feels himself to stand apart from the experience. Consequently, the whole notion of getting something out of life, of seeking from experience, becomes absurd. To put it in another way, it becomes vividly clear that in concrete fact I have no other self than the oneness of things of which I am aware.

Master Lin-Chi of the Tang dynasty said, "Just be ordinary and nothing special. Eat your food, move your bowels, pass water, and when you are tired, go and lie down. The ignorant will laugh at me, but the wise will understand." A person is not living a conceptually or scientifically defined life; for the essential quality of living life lies simply in the living. Do not, as when in the midst of enjoying yourself, step out for a moment and examine yourself to see if you are getting the utmost out of the occasion. Or not content with the happy feeling, you want to feel yourself feeling happy—so as to be sure not to miss anything.

Living exists when life lives through us—unhampered in its flow, for he who is living is not conscious of living and, in this, is the life he lives. Life lives; and in the living flow, no questions are raised. The reason is that life is a living now! Completeness, the now, is an absence of the conscious mind striving to divide that which is indivisible. For once the completeness of things is taken apart, it is no longer complete. All the pieces of a car that has been taken apart may be there, but it is no longer a car in its original nature, which is its function or life. So in order to live life whole-heartedly, the answer is, life simply is.

2-D

THE UNITY OF FIRMNESS AND SOFTNESS

Firmness (Yang) and gentleness (Yin) are two complementary and interdependent facets in the art of gung fu. It is because one singles out firmness and looks at it as distinct from softness that  *On the surface, softness and firmness appear to be opposites, but in reality they are inter-dependent—the complementary parts of a whole.*

the idea of "opposite" is formed. Once a distinction is made about something, that certain something will suggest its opposite.

On the surface, softness and firmness appear to be opposites, but in reality they are inter-dependent—the complementary parts of a whole. Their meaning (softness/firmness) is obtained FROM each other, and they find their completion THROUGH each other.

Source: Bruce Lee's handwritten paper entitled "The Union of Firmness and Softness." Bruce Lee Papers.

This "oneness" of things is a characteristic of the Chinese mind. In the Chinese language, events are looked on as a whole because their meanings are derived from each other. For example, the Chinese character for "good" and the Chinese character for "not good," when combined together will reflect the "quality" of something (whether good or not good). Likewise, the Chinese character for "long" and the Chinese character for "short," when brought together mean "length"; or the character for "buying" when combined with the character for "selling" forms the new word "trade."

All these examples show us that everything has a complementary part to form a whole. Now we can look at the "oneness" of firmness and softness, without favoring either side too

Not only does everything have a complementary part, but even within that "one" special thing it, too, should have the characteristic of the other component part. In other words, softness is to be concealed in firmness and firmness in softness.

much so that we can truly appreciate the "good/bad" of them. Not only does everything have a complementary part, but even within that "one" special thing it, too, should have the characteristic of the other component part. In other words, softness is to be concealed in firmness and firmness in softness. In either case, be it softness or firmness, it should never stand alone; for standing alone will lead to extremes and going to extremes is never best.

2-E

TAOISM

Taoism is a philosophy of the essential unity of the universe (monism), or reversion, polarization (Yin and Yang), and eternal cycles, of the leveling of all differences, the relativity of all standards, and the return of all to the primeval one, the divine intelligence, the source of all things.

From this philosophy naturally arises the absence of desire for strife and contention and fighting for advantage. Thus the teachings of humility and meekness of the Christian Sermon on the Mount find a rational basis, and a peaceable temper is bred in man. Taoism emphasizes nonresistance and the importance of gentleness.

The basic idea of the *Tao Te Ching* is NATURALISM in the sense of wu wei (inaction), which really means taking no unnatural action. It means spontaneity; that is, "to support all things in their natural stage" and thus allow them to "transform spontaneously." In this manner Tao "undertakes no activity and yet there is nothing left undone." In ordinary life it is expressed in "producing and rearing things without taking possession of them" and "doing work but not taking pride in it"—thus the natural Way stands in complement to all artificial ways such as regulation, ceremonies, and so forth. This is the reason that the Taoists don't like formalities and artificialities.

Source: Bruce Lee's typed notes entitled "Taoism," circa 1963. Bruce Lee Papers.

The natural way is compared with the ways of water. The female and the infant, that is the way of the weak. While there seems to be glorification of the weak, the strongest stress really lies with "simplicity." A simple life is one of plainness in which profit is discarded, cleverness abandoned, selfishness eliminated, and desires reduced. It is the life of "perfection which seems to be incomplete and of fullness which seems to be empty." It is the life that is as bright as light but does not dazzle. In short, it is a life of harmony, unity, contentment, tranquility, constancy, enlightenment, peace, and long life.

The basic idea of the Tao Te Ching is NATURALISM in the sense of wu wei (inaction), which really means taking no unnatural action. It means spontaneity; that is, "to support all things in their natural stage" and thus allow them to "transform spontaneously."

YIN-YANG

Harmony was regarded as the basic principle of the world order; as a cosmic field of force, in which the Yin and the Yang are eternally complementary and eternally changing. European dualism sees physical and metaphysical as two separate entities, at best as cause and effect, but never paired like sound and echo, or light and shadow, as in the Chinese symbol of all happening: the Yin and the Yang.

The dualistic philosophy reigned supreme in Europe, dominating the development of Western science. But with the advent of atomic physics, findings based on demonstrable experiments were seen to negate the dualistic theory, and the trend of thought since then has been back toward the monistic conception of the ancient Taoists.

In atomic physics no distinction is recognized between matter and energy; nor is it possible to make such a distinction, since they are in reality one essence, or at least two poles of the same unit. It is no longer possible, as it was in the mechanistic scientific era, to absolutely define weight, length, or time, and so forth, as the work of Einstein, Planck, Whitehead, and Jeans has demonstrated.

Source: Bruce Lee's typed note entitled "Yin-Yang," circa 1963. Bruce Lee Papers.

In the same way, the Taoist philosophy, against the background of which acupuncture had its origin and developed, is essentially monistic. The Chinese conceived the entire universe as activated by two principles, the Yang and the Yin, the positive and the negative, and they considered that nothing that exists, either animate or so-called inanimate, exists except by virtue of the ceaseless interplay of these two forces. Matter and energy, Yang and Yin, heaven and earth, are conceived of as essentially one or as two coexistent poles of one indivisible whole.

Gung fu, the oldest form of self-defense, can well be termed the concentrated essence of wisdom and profound thought on the art of self-defense. It has never been surpassed in terms of compre-hensiveness and depth of understanding. *Gung fu* means "training and discipline to discover the true Way to the object"—be it the way of health promotion, the way of spiritual cultivation, or the way of self-defense.

The object of gung fu, then, is to promote health, cultivate mind and self-protection. Its philosophy is based on the integral parts of the philosophies of Taoism, Chan (Zen), and the *I'Ching (Book of Changes)*—the ideal of giving with adversity, to bend slightly and spring back stronger than before, and to adapt oneself harmoni-ously to the opponent's movements without striving or resisting. Gung fu can be said to be the Chinese attempt to discover the mysteries of nature.

Harmony and calmness distinguish the Chinese art of gung fu. A gung fu man rejects all forms of self-assertiveness and competition, and he practices the art of self-forgetfulness—to detach not only from his opponent but from his "self."

Being yielding and devoted must not exclude having strength, for strength is necessary to the softness if it is to be the helper of the firmness. If the receptive were to push ahead on its own initiative, it would deviate from its natural character and miss the Way. By submitting to and following the creative, it attains its appropriate permanent place. Because the Receptive in its movement adapts itself to the Creative, these movements come to be. Thus the earth brings forth all beings, each in its own kind, according to the will of the Creator.

2-G

WU-HSIN (NO-MINDEDNESS)

The way of movement in gung fu is closely related to the movement of the mind. In fact, the mind is trained to direct the movement of the body. The mind wills and the body behaves.

The way of movement in gung fu is closely related to the movement of the mind In fact, the mind is trained to direct the movement of the body. The mind wills and the body behaves.

To perform the right technique in gung fu, physical loosening must be continued in a mental and spiritual loosening so as to make the mind not only agile but free. In order to accomplish this, a gung fu man has to remain quiet and calm and to master the principle of no-mindedness (wu-shin).

No-mindedness is not a blank mind that excludes all emotions; nor is it simply callousness and quietness of mind. Although quietude and calmness are necessary, it is the "non-graspiness" of the mind that mainly constitutes the principle of no-mindedness.

Source: Bruce Lee's handwritten essay entitled "No-Mindedness." Bruce Lee Papers.

A gung fu man employs his mind as a mirror—it grasps nothing, yet it refuses nothing; it receives, but does not keep. As Alan Watts puts it, the no-mindedness is "A state of wholeness in which the mind functions freely and easily, without the sensation of a second mind or ego standing over it with a club."[19] What he means is that one lets the mind think what it likes without the interference by the separate thinker or ego within oneself.

So long as it thinks what it wants, there is absolutely no effort in letting it go; and the disappearance of the effort to let go is precisely the disappearance of the separate thinker. There is nothing to try to do, for whatever comes up moment by moment is accepted, including nonacceptance. No-mindedness is then not being without emotion or feeling, but being one in whom feeling is not sticky or blocked. It is a mind immune to emotional influences. "Like this river, everything is flowing on ceaselessly without cessation or standing still."

No-mindedness is employing the whole mind as we use the eyes when we rest them upon various objects but make no special effort to take anything in. Chuang-tzu, the disciple of Lao-tzu, stated:

> The baby looks at things all day without winking, that is because his eyes are not focused on any particular object. He goes without knowing where he is going, and stops without knowing what he is doing. He merges himself with the surroundings and moves along with it. These are the principles of mental hygiene.[20]

Therefore, concentration in gung fu does not have the usual sense of restricting the attention to a single sense object, but is simply a quiet awareness of whatever happens to be here and now. Such quiet awareness can be illustrated by an audience at a football game; instead of a concentrated attention on the player that has the ball, they have an awareness of the whole football field.

In a similar way, a gung fu man's mind is concentrated by not dwelling on any particular part of the opponent. This is especially true when one is dealing with more than one or two opponents. For instance, suppose ten men are attacking a person, each in succession, ready to strike him down. As soon as one is disposed of, he will move on to another without permitting the mind to "stop" with any. However rapidly the blows may follow one upon another he leaves no time to intervene between the two. Every one of the ten will thus be successively and successfully dealt with. This is possible only when the mind moves from one object to another without being "stopped" or arrested by anything. If the mind is unable to flow on in this fashion, it is sure to lose the combat somewhere between two encounters.

A gung fu man's mind is present everywhere because it is nowhere attached to any particular object. And it can remain present because even when related to this

A gung fu man's mind is present everywhere because it is nowhere attached to any particular object. And it can remain present because even when related to this or that object it does not cling to it.

or that object, it does not cling to it. The flow of thought is like water filling a pond, which is always ready to flow off again. It can work its inexhaustible power because it is free, and it can be open to everything because it is empty. This can be compared with what Chang Chen Chi called "Serene Reflection": "Serene means tranquility of no thought, and reflection means vivid and clear awareness. Therefore, serene reflection is clear awareness of no thought."[21]

Not to localize or partialize is the end of spiritual training. Wwhen it is nowhere attached it is everywhere. When it occupies one-tenth, it is absent in the other nine-tenths. The gung fu man should discipline himself to have the mind go on its own way, instead of trying deliberately to confine it somewhere.

2-H

WU WEI (NON-ACTION)

A gung fu man aims at harmony with himself and his opponent. To be in harmony with his opponent is possible not through force, which provokes conflicts and reactions, but through a yielding to his force.

In other words, a gung fu man promotes the spontaneous development of his opponent and does not venture to interfere by his own action. He loses himself by giving up all subjective feelings and individuality, and by becoming one with his opponent. Inside his mind, oppositions have become mutually cooperative instead of mutually exclusive. When his private ego and conscious effort yield to a power that is not his own, he then achieves the highest action in gung fu, the action of no action—wu wei.

Wu means "not" or "non," and *wei* means "action," "doing," "striving," "straining," or "busyness." However, it doesn't really mean doing nothing, but to let one's mind alone, trusting it to work by itself. The most important thing is not to strain in any way.

Wu wei, in gung fu, means "spirit or mind action," in the sense that the governing force is the mind, not the senses. During sparring a gung fu man learns to forget about himself and follows the movement of his opponent, leaving his mind free to make its own countermovement without any interfering deliberation. He frees himself from all mental suggestions of resistance and adopts a supple attitude. His actions are all performed without self-assertion; he lets his mind remain spontaneous and ungrasped. As soon as he stops to think, his flow of movement will be disturbed, and he will immediately be struck by his opponent. Every action, therefore, has to be done "unintentionally" without ever trying.

The natural phenomenon with the closest resemblance to wu wei is water: Water is the softest substance in the world, yet it can penetrate the hardest. Water is so fine that it is impossible to grasp a handful of it; strike it, yet it does not suffer hurt; stab it, and it is not wounded; sever it, yet it is not divided. It has no shape of its own, but molds itself to the receptacle that contains it.

Source: Bruce Lee's handwritten essay entitled "Wu Wei." Bruce Lee Papers.

Wu wei is the art of artlessness, the principle of no-principle. To state it in terms of gung fu, the genuine beginner knows nothing about the way of blocking and striking, and much less

Wu wei is the art of artlessness, the principle of no-principle. To state it in terms of gung fu, the genuine beginner knows nothing about the way of y blocking and striking, and much less of his concern for himself.

of his concern for himself. When the opponent tries to strike him, he instinctively blocks it. This is all he can do. But as soon as the training starts, he is taught how to defend and attack, where to keep his mind, and many other technical skills—which make his mind "stop" at various junctures. For this reason whenever he tries to strike the opponent he feels unusually hampered. He has lost altogether his original sense of purity and freedom. But as months and years go by, as his training acquires fuller maturity, his bodily attitude and his way of managing the techniques toward no-mind-edness, will resemble the state of mind he had at the very beginning of training when he knew nothing, when he was altogether ignorant of gung fu.

The beginning and the end thus turn into next-door neighbors. In the musical scale, one may start with the lowest pitch and gradually ascend to the highest. When the highest is reached, one finds it is located next to the lowest. In a similar way, when the highest stage is reached in the study of gung fu, a gung fu man turns into a kind of simpleton who knows nothing of gung fu and is devoid of all learning. He loses sight of intellectual calculations, and a state of no-mindedness prevails.

When the ultimate perfection is attained, the body and limbs perform by themselves what is assigned to them to do with no interference from the mind. The technical skill is so automatic it is completely divorced from the conscious efforts. That's why the Chinese say the highest skill is done on an almost unconscious level.

THE LETTING-GO

It exists HERE and NOW; it requires only one thing to see it: openness, freedom—the freedom to be open and not tethered by any ideas, concepts, and so forth. We can go on rehearsing, analyzing, attending lectures, and so forth, until we are blue in the face; all this will [not] be [of] the slightest avail—it is only when we stop thinking and let go that we can start seeing, discovering.

When our mind is tranquil, there will be an occasional pause to its feverish activities, there will be a letting go, and it is only then in the interval between two thoughts that a flash of UNDERSTAND-ING—understanding, which is not thought— can take place.

Source: Bruce Lee's handwritten essay entitled "The Letting-Go," circa 1960. this piece was discovered pressed between pages 120 and 121 in the chapter entitled "Spirituality, Sensuality" of the book *This Is It* by Alan Watts, published in 1960, by Pantheon Books, New York. Lee had inscribed his Jefferson Avenue, Seattle address inside the front page.

2-J

ON WESTERN PHILOSOPHY

The process of philosophy is to get or obtain clear information on virtually any topic, but certain philosophers, such as Plato, have as their focal point the realm of ethics and morality. Specifically, issues that deal with "good" and "bad," what constitutes the "ideal life" that one ought to strive for.

Plato, through the character of Socrates, has a specific method of presenting his position on a given topic. His method of argument comprising three steps:

1. starting with certain premises,
2. going through a process of reasoning, leading his opponent to
3. his conclusion.

The only way to dismantle the so-called Socratic method of argument is also a three-step process:

1. if the truth of the first is challenged successfully,
2. and if the remaining premises that are based on the original premise follow logically,
3. the conclusion is false.

Source: Bruce Lee's handwritten notes entitled "Philosophy," found in Bruce Lee's philosophy notebook University of Washington, dated January 7, 1963. Bruce Lee Papers.

PLATO

The Greek Philosopher Plato (c. 428 B.C-C.348 B.C.) believed that education was the key to everything. His position was that, once someone mastered justice, he would act justly; whereas one who acts unjust, does so simply because he is unaware of what the alternative is.

According to Plato, everyone strives to be good in nature and, ultimately, all deeds lead to something good. Plato believed that moral knowledge is possible.

According to Plato, everyone strives to be good in nature and, ultimately, all deeds lead to something good. Plato believed that moral knowledge is possible.

Source: Bruce Lee's handwritten notes entitled "Plato," found in Bruce Lee's philosophy notebook, University of Washington, dated January 7, 1963. Bruce Lee Papers.

2-L

PLATO'S "GORGIAS"

Author: Plato

Type of Work: Philosophy of Rhetoric, Ethics.

The Concept and Principal Ideas Advanced: Socrates and Gorgias discuss the question concerning the use of rhetoric, and Socrates initiates the discussion by describing rhetoric as the "art of persuasion." But, Socrates argues, if the rhetorician has no knowledge of what he proclaims, it is a case of the ignorant attempting to teach the ignorant; furthermore, if he discourses on justice, he must have knowledge of justice, and if he has knowledge of justice, he is just. Consequently, he could not tolerate the unjust, which would be talking without having knowledge of what one was talking about.

According to Socrates, since all men desire to act for the sake of some good, no man can act as he wills if he acts in ignorance of the good; if a man acts wrongly, he acts in ignorance of the evil

According to Socrates, since all men desire to act for the sake of some good, no man can act as he wills if he acts in ignorance of the good; if man acts wrongly, he acts in ignorance of the evil that he does.

that he does. Consequently, punishment should aim at rehabilitation, and it is better to be punished for one's misdeeds than to escape punishment.

From all this, Socrates argues, it follows that the art of rhetoric should be used to make men aware of injustice and of the cure for injustice. Callicles argues that natural justice is the rule of the stronger, but Socrates suggests that the wise are the strong; Callicles then argues that the wise man seeks pleasure for himself, but Socrates shows that pleasure and pain are not identical with the good and the bad.

Source: Bruce Lee's handwritten notes entitled "Plato's Gorgias," found in Bruce Lee's philosophy notebook, University of Washington, dated January 7, 1963. Bruce Lee Papers.

SOCRATES

Socrates has led Callicles to go along with him that good is the opposite of evil and the two cannot exist at the same time and at the same place. Pain and pleasure, on the other hand, can be otherwise, because when a man is extremely thirsty, which is painful, he needs water to drink, which is pleasure.

During the moment of drinking the water (when he is thirsty) he experiences both pain and pleasure. It shows, then, that good cannot be compared with pleasure or evil with pain (the same way is true that a bad man and a good man can both feel pleasure and pain to various degrees) because they are not co-existing.

Good and bad or pleasure and pain exist but for the other. Instead of opposites, they are complementaries and are a function each of the other. First of all, if I have not felt pain how can I distinguish pleasure, or vice versa?

Looking at the sky I can distinguish a smaller star because of the big stars, and if there were no black sky at all, there would be no stars. It is not a matter to struggle between the good and the bad, but to flow like waves on the water.

Looking at the sky I can distinguish a smaller star because of the big stars, and if there were no black sky at all, there would be no stars. It is not a matter to struggle between the good and the bad, but to flow like waves on the water.

Source: Bruce Lee's handwritten philosophy essay entitled "Socrates," University of Washington, circa 1964. Bruce Lee Papers.

2-N

THE NATURE OF HUMANKIND

The measure of the moral worth of a man is his happiness. The better the man, the more happiness. Happiness is the synonym of well-being. Further, the worth of a man, in turn, influences what his job should be. Once he functions the way he ought to, he is happy.

- What is the right (that is, just, ethical, moral) conduct for a man?
- A human being is a (eat, sleep, physical) maintaining, reproducing entity.
- A human being is an entity of feeling.
- A human being is a creating entity.

In fact, it is the creative ability of a human being that separates him from all other animals. Right conduct is governed by reason and creativity.

Source: Bruce Lee's handwritten notes, untitled, found in Bruce Lee's philosophy note-book, University of Washington, dated January 7, 1963. Bruce Lee Papers.

2-0

MORAL CONDUCT: RELATIVE VERSUS ABSOLUTE

1. To hold moral conduct as absolute might be to hold that action can be described in any old way.
2. It might be to hold that action described in a certain way is applicable to all at all times.
3. To hold it as relative might be to hold that it applies as a function of time, geographic climate, social and economical needs, religious beliefs, and so forth.
4. To hold it as relative might be to hold that the expression of right conduct might mean right conduct is the dictate of public interest, and so forth.
5. To hold it as absolute might be to hold that expressing right conduct can be defined invariably.

Source: Bruce Lee's handwritten notes entitled "Moral Conduct: Relative Versus Absolute," found in Bruce Lee's philosophy notebook, University of Washington, dated January 13, 1963. Bruce Lee Papers.

Artist of Life

2-P

OBJECTIVE AND SUBJECTIVE JUDGMENTS

1. A judgment is objective if it concerns objective questions; a subjective judgment is one which concerns one's personal view on the objective.
2. Objective is factual. Subjective is a matter of opinion.
3. There is a big difference between why you THINK something is wrong and to justify, explain, prove that something is wrong.
4. A concept is objective if the quality denoted is the actual quality of action (inherent in the objective).

Everybody is capable of obtaining happiness, but the matter of going on, or taking action to obtain it, is in question.

Source: Bruce Lee's handwritten notes entitled "Objective and Subjective Judgments," found in Bruce Lee's philosophy notebook, University of Washington, dated January 13, 1963. Bruce Lee Papers.

2-Q
RENE DESCARTES

The French philosopher and mathematician Rene Descartes (1591-1650) is known primarily for his epistemology. Epistemology is considered the "philosophy of

The skeptic really cannot be debated. Things should be absolutely reasonable and justifiable before one can accept them. If you can doubt things, then they are not too stable.

knowledge" and is concerned with issues such as how and what do we know? His epistemological position arose to combat the skeptics—those who think people cannot (do not) know anything with any certainty. Skepticism, as Descartes saw it, was generated by two questions:

1. How do you know that?
2. What makes you think you really know that (that is, why is it a good reason)?

The skeptic really cannot be debated. Things should be absolutely reasonable and justifiable before one can accept them. If you can doubt things, then they are not too stable.

Dream—a false representation

Hallucination—a false general sensory or mental representation

It is possible for us to misinterpret the vision of the world.

Source: Bruce Lee's handwritten notes entitled "Descartes" found in his philosophy notebook, dated January 13, 1963, and January 23, 1963, University of Washington. Bruce Lee Papers.

2-R

DESCARTES'S "MEDITATIONS"

Author: Rene Descartes
Type of Work: Epistemology
Meditations (1641)

1. Gives views on the absolute distinction of mind/body.
2. Body subject to mechanical causal laws.
3. Mind is free from mechanical causal laws and exists independently.
4. This distinction is Descartes's purpose of showing that the doctrines of the Catholic faith are reconcilable with progress and discovery in the physical sciences.
5. Meditations are Descartes's most important philosophical work, containing his chief metaphysical teaching.

Meditation One (Outline)

In the first of these meditations, Descartes offers reasons for his methodological skepticism:

1. Doubt is useful, since it frees us from prejudice.
2. Doubt shows how the mind may escape from the senses.
3. Doubt makes it impossible for us ever to doubt those things that we have once discovered to be true.

Concerning What May Be Doubted

1. Descartes wanted to get rid of all old beliefs, even those that were not all false or not yet proven to be false.
2. All he considered true was based upon sense perception— "learned either from the senses or through the senses."

Source: Bruce Lee's handwritten notes entitled "Descartes Meditations," found in his Philosophy notebook, dated January 13, 1963, and January 23, 1963, University of Washington. Bruce Lee Papers.

3. Although the senses are often deceptive, Descartes yet realizes many things one learns by his senses can be reasonably sure (the fact that he was seated where he was when writing his Meditation, for example).
4. Yet we believe things are real while we are only dreaming them.
5. Can we then be sure that right now is not an illusion (a dream)?
6. According to Descartes, God is the Perfect Being who would not allow us to be deceived.
7. Yet we can be and sometimes are deceived.
8. Why should a God who could not allow us always to be deceived, allow us to be deceived sometimes?
9. Descartes invokes the idea of a malignant demon who may be supposed to be doing his best to mislead men into falsehood. (Note: A more serious answer to the problem is found in the fourth meditation, where Descartes argues that it is a wrong use of man's free will that leads him into error; that by arrogantly making up his mind to a judgment where there are in sufficient reasons to support it, he brings false-hood upon himself. For error, as for moral wickedness, God is not responsible. By the first suggestion, the blame was on the devil; by this, it is on the man. Only by setting ourselves to accept nothing but what is, by the Cartesian criterion, genuinely acceptable, we will avoid error.)
10. At the end of his first meditation, Descartes continues to live in a state of suspended judgment.

According to Descartes
1. The mind and body can be separated.
2. The mind can do away with the body (Cartesian dualism).
3. The thing he can't doubt is his existence. He has to be there (that is, to exist) to doubt whether he is in a dream or is being deceived by the demon (at least he supposes he is there).
4. Therefore, he concludes, there exists no doubt of one's existence ("I think, therefore I am").

Meditation Three (The Demonstration of the Existence of God)

Two forms of argument are presented:

1. First, he asks directly concerning the IDEA of a perfect being, whence it could have come into his mind: from some other creature? From himself? Or must there exist a perfect being to originate the idea? His answer is obscured for the modern reader by the late-medieval philosophical frame work in which it is expressed. According to Descartes, the idea of God contains more "objective reality" than any other idea (including my idea of myself). But a more perfect idea cannot be generated by a less perfect being. Therefore, concludes Descartes, the idea of God in his mind must have been placed there by God himself.

2. The second form of the argument proceeds from the contingent quality of his own existence, made up as it is of fleeting instants, no one of which is able either to conserve itself or to engender its successor. Much in the argument reminds one of the traditional Aristotelian proof; but there is this difference which makes it clear that the new argument is only another version of the first—it is not merely the existence of a contingent being that has to be explained, or of a thinking being, but of "a being which thinks and which has some idea of God." Thus the principle that there must be at least as much reality in the cause as in the effect precludes the possibility that any being less perfect than God could have created Descartes—or any man.

DESCARTES—AN OPINION

Descartes believes that some ideas are innate, some are from the outside, and still some others are the combination of both. He decides to consider those ideas proceeding from external objects and to find out what are the reasons that cause him to think that these ideas of things (which he has) are similar to the things themselves.

He believes that the things outside are not caused by his imagination, for when the fire makes him feel hot, the feeling of heat is imprinted on him involuntarily whether he likes it or not. Nature works the same way; however, nature can

Descartes believes that some ideas are innate, some are from the outside, and still some others are the combination of both. He decides to consider those ideas proceeding from external objects and to find out what are the reasons that cause him to think that these ideas of things (which he has) are similar to the things themselves.

lead man astray because in the active choosing between vice and virtue, Descartes thinks that most men would choose the former. Perhaps we only imagine the existence of these external objects of which we have ideas, and even if these ideas he has do proceed from the external objects, which are different from himself, it still does not prove that the idea he has resembles any objects in nature. On the contrary, there is often a great difference in the sun (there is only one right one). Descartes concludes that "it was not by a certain judgment."

Source: Bruce Lee's handwritten notes entitled "Descartes" found in his philosophy notebook, dated January 13, 1963, and January 23, 1963, University of Washington. Bruce Lee Papers.

Artist of Life

2-T

ON DESCARTES'S "COGITO"

"Cogito, ergo sum," Descartes's dictum, which, when translated from the French reads, "I think, therefore I am," can [really] only mean, "I think, therefore I am a thinker." This being of the "I am," which is deduced from "I think," is merely a knowing.

This being knowledge, but not life. And the primary reality is not what I think, but that I live, for those also live who do not think. Although this living may not be a real living. God! What contradictions when we seek to join in wedlock life and reason!

The truth is *"Sum, ergo cogito"*—"I am, therefore I think," although not everything that is, thinks. Is not conscious thinking above all consciousness of being? Is pure thought possible, without consciousness of self, without personality? Can there exist pure knowledge without feeling, without that species of materiality which feeling lends to it? Do we not perhaps feel thought, and do we not feel ourselves in the act of knowing and willing?

The defect of Descartes's discourse On Method lies in his resolution to begin by emptying himself of himself—of Descartes, of the real man, the man of flesh and bone, the man who does not want to die—in order that he might be a mere thinker—that is, an abstraction. But the real man returned and thrust himself into his philosophy.

The defect of Descartes's discourse On Method lies in his resolution to begin by emptying himself of himself—of Descartes, of the real man, the man of flesh and bone, the man who does not want to die,— in order that he might be a mere thinker,— that is, an abstraction.

Source: Bruce Lee's handwritten essay "Descartes," University of Washington, January 24, 1964, and Bruce Lee's handwritten notes entitled "Cogito Ergo Sum," from his philosophy notebook, dated January 7, 1964. Bruce Lee Papers.

2-U

"ANY COLOR I WANT"

"Take the paint out of this can and you may paint the room any color you want." This quotation was one of the first things I heard in a conversation with one of my fellow Chinese friends when I mentioned the name of Thomas Aquinas.

I am sure the quotation was not his creation, but what followed was most certainly his own interpretation: if an individual is willing to accept a first premise in any philosophical system, then what follows from that premise must also be accepted.

And so to Thomas Aquinas and his third article on the existence of God from the *Summa Theologica.*

The Five Proofs

- "It is impossible that in the same respect and in the way a thing should be both mover and moved; that is, that is should move itself... Therefore it is necessary to arrive at a first mover, moved by no other; and this everyone understands to be God."
- "It is necessary to admit a first efficient cause, to which everyone gives the name of God."
- "We cannot admit of the existence of some being having of itself its own necessity, and not receiving it from another, but rather causing in others their necessity. This all men speak of as God."
- (Gradation, or from more to less.) "There must also be something which is to all beings the cause of their being, goodness, and every other perfection; and this we call God."
- (Intelligence, that is, impossibility of chance or purpose.) "Some intelligent being exists by whom all natural things are directed to their end; and this being we call God."[22]

Source: Bruce Lee's handwritten philosophy essay entitled "Any Color I Want?" University of Washington, circa 1964. Bruce Lee Papers.

Artist of Life

The above argument for the existence of God rests on the first premise, or "proof" as it is called. Thus, and hence and consequently and therefore, if one removes the first premise of Aquinas on Motion, one is trapped into the second premise on Efficient Cause, and so to the third, fourth, and fifth arguments.

What is disturbing about these arguments (despite the fact that my early schooling in Hong Kong was directed along these lines by Roman Catholic priests) is the overwhelming fact that I can either accept them or reject them regardless of their validity.

To experience pain, for example, does not necessarily mean that one understands it, accepts it, or even for that matter denies its existence: It is. But it does not follow that everyone will understand pain in the same way and arrive at the same conclusion. All one has to do is take a close look at the medical profession.

However, when I say that pain "is," it does imply that I am experiencing some THING, but to relate this THING to someone other than myself seems to be where the

To experience pain, for example, does not necessarily mean that one understands it, accepts it, or even for that matter denies its existence: It is. But it does not follow that everyone will understand pain in the same way and arrive at the same conclusion.

difficulty lies. It is, I believe, more than a semantic difficulty—it is impossibility. Semantically we all respond to a given idea, concept, or word in much the same way: that is, if the concept, idea or word is in our own native language.

However, when a Western man reasons, he makes distinctions that would be impossible for the Chinese man to make—in fact, the Chinese would not even consider "distinction" as a part of their thought process. The Chinese looks at things as essentially ONE, or as two coexistent parts of one indivisible whole. Their meaning (whatever the things happen to be) is derived from each other and their completion through each other. Therefore, instead of mutually exclusive, they are mutually dependent and are a function each of the other.

In the Chinese language, for instance, events are looked on as a whole; therefore it is impossible to try to think of a cause and effect relationship. For example, the character for "good" is 好 and that of "bad" 壞. When combined together 好壞 the word *quality* is formed. In order to form the whole word *quality,* half of the positive of 好 is necessary. 長 is the character for "long," and 短, the character for "short," and together it *(long/short)* means the length of something. The character for "buying" 買 and that for "selling," 賣 combine together to form the new word *trade.*

Instead of being opposite to each other, things are complementary, and complementaries coexist. They are not viewed as cause and effect but are paired like sound and echo or light and shadow. So in order for a bicyclist to move forward the one inseparable force of one's unceasing interplay of pumping and releasing is required.

Now when Aquinas begins his argument he presupposes Being or Existence, for to talk in terms of motion implies that something exists; that is, [that] some thing is in motion. What Aquinas is asking, then, in Article Three, is for me to accept from his "can of paint" the absolute being that he conceives of as God.

I prefer to look upon Aquinas's doctrine as an act of faith rather than "reason." I cannot and will not "scoff" at faith when reason seems to be such a barren thing. The Chinese realize that the highest truth is inexpressible, and instead to strive, to presuppose, to separate self they cease all seeking and all mind activity in the nature of clinging or grasping directed at self-assertion or spiritual gain; he simply is being what is.

Part 3

PSYCHOLOGY

Given that it was his mind that separated Bruce Lee from every other martial artist (and, for that matter, every other human being) of his era, it should not surprise us to learn that the mind and its functioning were areas of immense interest to him.

The library of Lee's home contained many books on psychology and psychotherapy by the leading figures in the field. Although Lee never considered himself qualified to discourse on such matters, his study time in the area of mental health was considerable. Many were the hours Lee spent in the company (via the printed page) of men such as Carl Jung, Carl Rogers, and Frederick S. Perls, the founder of Gestalt therapy.

The results of the research these individuals conducted with hundreds (in some cases thousands) of clinical patients had a huge impact on Lee's own thought process, and many of their views (most notably those of Perls, which are included in this section) he transcribed verbatim, adopting them, en toto, both as a means to understand himself better as a human being, and also as an aid to assist his martial art student: in coming to know themselves.

As a direct result of Lee's research into the field of psychology, he was able to further expand his intellect and bring a deeper understanding to bear on his personal and social relationships.

NOTES ON GESTALT THERAPY

Health is an appropriate balance of the coordination of all of what we "are" (are is being mind rather than having mind).

An organism works as a whole. We are not a summation of part, but a very subtle coordination of all these different bits that go into the making of the organism—we HAVE not a liver or a heart. We ARE liver and heart and brain and so on.

To promote the growth process and develop human potential:

a. to get through social role playing

b. to fill in the holes in the personality to make whole and complete again.

Anxiety is the excitement we carry with us and which becomes stagnated, bottled up, if we are unsure about the role we have to play—we hesitate, our hearts begin to race and all the excitement can't flow into activity, and we have stage fright—ANXIETY—the gap between the NOW and the THEN. So if you are in the NOW, you are creative, you are inventive. If you are in the NOW, you can't be anxious, because your excitement flows immediately into ongoing spontaneous activity.

Anxiety is the excitement we carry with us and which becomes stagnated, bottled up, if we are unsure about the role we have to play—we hesitate, our hearts begin to race and all the excitement can't flow into activity, and we have stage fright.

The meaning of life is that it is to be lived, and it is not to be traded and conceptualized and squeezed into a pattern of systems. We realize that manipulation and control are not the ultimate joy of life—to become real, to learn to take a stand, to develop one's center, to support our total personality, a release to spontaneity—yes, yes, yes.

Source: Bruce Lee's handwritten notes entitled "Notes on Gestalt Therapy," within Misc. Notes. Bruce Lee Papers.

I do my thing, and you do your thing.
I am not in this world to live up to your expectations.
And you are not in this world to live up to mine.
You are you and I am I,
And if by chance we find each other, it's beautiful.
If not, it can't be helped.

Once you have a character, you have developed a rigid SYSTEM. Your behavior becomes petrified, predictable, and you lose your ability to cope freely with the world with all your resources. You are

We realize that manipulation and control are not the ultimate joy of life—to become real, to learn to take a stand, to develop one's center, to support our total personality, a release to spontaneity—yes, yes, yes.

predetermined just to cope with events in one way, namely, as your character prescribes. So it seems a paradox when I say that the richest person, the most productive, creative person, is a person who has NO CHARACTER. In our society, we DEMAND that a person have a character, and especially a "good" character, because then he is predictable, and he can be pigeonholed, and so on.

3-B

THE RELATIONSHIP OF THE ORGANISM TO ITS ENVIRONMENT

The Ego Boundary. The ego boundary is not a fixed thing. If it is fixed, then it again becomes character, or an armor, like on the turtle. The ego boundary is the differentiation between the self and the other.

1. The two phenomena of the ego boundary are identification and alienation.
2. So inside the ego boundary, there is generally cohesion, love, cooperation; outside the ego boundary there is suspicion, strangeness, unfamiliarity.
3. The polarity of attraction and rejection: of appetite and disgust. There is always a polarity going on, and inside the boundary we have the feeling of familiarity, of right; outside is strangeness, and wrong. Inside is good and bad; right and wrong is always a matter of boundary, of which side of the fence I am on.
4. The wish to change is based upon the phenomenon of dissatisfaction. Every time you want to change yourself, or you want to change environment, the basis always is dissatisfaction.
5. Hate is a function of kicking somebody out of the boundary for something—alienation, disowning.

Source: Bruce Lee's handwritten notes entitled "Relationship of the Organism to Its Environment," within *Misc. Notes.* Bruce Lee Papers.

If some of our thoughts, feelings, are unacceptable to us, we want to disown them. There are many of these kinds of ways to remain intact, but always only at the cost of disowning many, many valuable parts of ourselves. The fact that we live only on such a small percentage of our potential is due to the fact that we are not willing—or society or whatever you want to call it, is not willing—to accept myself, yourself, as the organism that you are by birth, constitution, and so on.

You do not allow yourself—or you are not allowed—to be totally yourself. So your ego boundary shrinks more and more. Your power, your energy becomes smaller and smaller. Your ability to cope with the world becomes less and less—and more and more rigid, more and more allowed only to cope as your character, as your preconceived pattern, prescribes it.

A living organism is an organism that consists of thousands and thousands of processes that require interchange with other media outside the boundary of the organism. So something has to happen to get through the boundary, and this is what we call contact.

We touch, we get in contact, and we stretch our boundary out to the thing in question. If we are rigid and can't move, then it remains there.

When we live, we spend energies; we need energies to maintain this machine. This process of exchange is called the metabolism. Both the metabolism of the exchange of our organism with the environment, and the metabolism within our organism, is going on continually, day and night.

A gestalt is an organic function (walking—thirst—walking)—this situation is now closed, and the next unfinished situation can take place, which means our life is basically practically nothing but an infinite number of unfinished situations—incomplete gestalts. No sooner have we finished one situation than another comes up.

THREE TYPES OF PHILOSOPHY

1. *Aboutism.* We talk about it and talk about it, and nothing is accomplished. In scientific explanation, you usually go around and around and never touch the heart of the matter.

2. *Shouldism.* You should be this, you should change yourself, you should not do this—a hundred thousand commands, but no consideration is given to what degree the person who "should" do this can actually comply. And furthermore, most people expect that the magic formula, just to use the sounds, "You should do this," might have an actual effect on reality.

3. *Existentialism.* Existentialism wants to do away with concepts and to work on the awareness principle, on phenomenology. The setback with the present existentialist philosophies is that they need their support from somewhere else. If you look at the existentialists, they say that they are nonconceptual, but if you look at the people, they all borrow concepts from other sources. Buber from Judaism, Tillich from Protestantism, Sartre from Socialism, Heidegger from language, Binswanger from psychoanalysis.

Gestalt therapy tries to be in harmony, in alignment, with everything else, with medicine, with science, with the universe, with what is.

Gestalt therapy is the first existential philosophy that stands on its own feet. It has its support in its own formation because the Gestalt formation, the emergence of the needs, is a primary biological phenomenon. Gestalt therapy tries to be in harmony, in alignment, with everything else, with medicine, with science, with the universe, with what is.

Source: Bruce Lee's handwritten notes entitled "Three Types of Philosophy," contained within *Misc. Notes.* Bruce Lee Papers.

An organism is a system that is in balance and that has to function properly. Any imbalance is experienced as a need to correct this imbalance. Now, practically, we have hundreds of unfinished

An organism is a system that is in balance and that has to function properly. Any imbalance is experienced as a need to correct this imbalance. Now, practically we have hundreds of unfinished situations in us.

situations in us. How come we are not completely confused and want to go out in all directions?

And that's another observation that I have discovered, that, from the survival point of view, the most urgent situation becomes the controller, the director, and takes over.

The most urgent situation emerges, and in any case of emergency, you realize that this has to take precedence over any other activity (for example, running from a sudden fire—out of breath to rest for oxygen supply—run again).

3-D

SELF-REGULATION VERSUS EXTERNAL REGULATION

The important thing to remember and to understand is that AWARENESS, per se— by itself and of itself—can be curative. Because with full awareness you become aware of this organismic self-regu- lation; you can let the organ-

Because with full awareness you become aware of this organismic self-regulation; you can let the organism take over without interfering, without interrupting; we can rely on the wisdom of the organism.

ism take over without interfering, without interrupting; we can rely on the wisdom of the organism. And the contrast to this is the whole pathology of self-manipulation, environmental control, and so on, which interferes with this subtle organismic self-control.

Our manipulation of ourselves is usually dignified by the word "conscience," which is nothing but a fantasy, a projection onto the parents. The "road to hell is paved with good intentions," and any intention toward idealistic change will achieve the opposite—the New Year's resolutions, the desperation of trying to be different, the attempt to control oneself, and so forth.

Source: Bruce Lee's handwritten notes entitled "Self-Regulation versus External Regulation," contained within *Misc. Notes.* Bruce Lee Papers.

If we are willing to stay in the center of our world, and not have the center either in our computer or somewhere else, but really in the center, then we are ambidextrous—then we see the two poles of every event. We see that light cannot exist without non-light. If there is same-ness, you can't be aware anymore. If there is always light, you don't experience light anymore. You have to have the rhythm of light and darkness.

If we are willing to stay in the center of our world, and not have the center either in our computer or somewhere else, but really in the center, then we are ambidextrous—then we see the two poles of every event.

THE TOP DOG AND THE UNDERDOG

If we examine the two clowns—the top dog and the underdog— that perform the self-torture game on the stage of our fantasy, then we usually find the two characters to be like this:

The Top Dog

The top dog usually is righteous and authoritarian; he knows best. He is sometimes right, but always righteous. The top dog is a bully and works with "you should" and "you should not." The top dog manipulates with demands and threats of catastrophe, such as, "If you don't ... then— you won't be loved, you won't get to heaven, you will die," and so on.

The Underdog

The underdog manipulates with being defensive, apologetic, wheedling, playing the crybaby, and such. The underdog has no power. The underdog is Mickey Mouse. The top dog is the super-mouse. And the underdog works like this: "I try my best," "Look, I try again and again. I can't help it if I fail." "I have such good intentions." So you see the underdog is cunning, and he usually gets the better of the top dog because the underdog is not as primitive as the top dog. So the top dog and underdog strive for control. Like every parent and child, they strive with each other for control. The person is fragmented into controller and controlled. This inner conflict, the struggle between the top dog and underdog, is never complete, because the top dog as well as the underdog fights for his life.

This is the basis for the famous self-torture game. We usually take for granted that the top dog is right, and in many cases the top dog makes impossible perfectionistic demands. So if you are cursed with perfectionism, then you're absolutely sunk. This ideal

Source: Bruce Lee's handwritten notes entitled "The Top Dog and the Underdog," within Misc. Notes. Bruce Lee Papers.

is a yardstick which always gives you the opportunity to brow-beat yourself, to berate yourself and others. Since this ideal is an impossibility, you can never live up to it. You are merely in love with this ideal, and there is no end to the self-torture, to the self-nagging, self-castigating. It hides under the mask of "self-improvement." It never works.

If the person tries to meet the top dog's demands of perfectionism, the result is a "nervous breakdown," or flight into insanity. This is one of the tools of the underdog. Once we recognize the structure of our behavior, *which in the case of self-improvement is the split between the top dog and the underdog,* and understand how, by listening, we can bring about a reconciliation of these two fighting clowns, then we realize that we cannot deliberately bring about changes in ourselves or in others.

This is a very decisive point: MANY PEOPLE DEDICATE THEIR LIVES TO ACTUALIZING A CONCEPT OF WHAT THEY SHOULD BE LIKE, RATHER THAN ACTUALIZING THEMSELVES. This difference between SELF-ACTUALIZ-ING and SELF-IMAGE ACTUALIZING is *very* important. Most people only live for their image.

Where some people have a self, most people have a void, be-cause they are so busy PROJECTING themselves as this or that. This is again the curse of the ideal. The curse is that you should not be what you are. Every external control, even internalized external control—"you should"—interferes with the healthy working of the organism. There is only one thing that should control the situation. *If you understand the situation that you are in, and let the situation that you are in control your actions, then you learn how to cope with life.* For example, you don't drive according to the program, you drive according to the situation (same thing in combat). You drive a different speed when you are tired, when it's raining, and so forth. The less confident we are in ourselves, the less we are in touch with ourselves and the world, the more we want to control.

NOW = EXPERIENCE = AWARENESS = REALITY

Gestalt therapy = phenomenological approach (awareness of what is) + behavioral approach (behavior in the now).

THE FOUR BASIC PHILOSOPHICAL APPROACHES

Aboutism keeps out any emotional responses or other genuine involvement—as though we were things. In therapy, Aboutism is found in rationalization and intellectualization, and in the "interpretation" games where the therapist says, "This is what your difficulties are about." This approach is based on noninvolvement.

With *Shouldism* you grow up completely surrounded by what you should and should not do, and you spend much of your time playing this game within yourself—the game I call the "Top Dog/Underdog Game" or the "self-improvement game" or the "self-torture game." Shouldism is based on the phenomenon of dissatisfaction.

The *Existential* ("is-ism") approach is the eternal attempt to achieve truth, but what is truth? Truth is one of what I call the "fitting games."

Gestalt attempts to understand the existence of any event through the way it comes about, which tries to understand becoming by the how, not the why; through the all-pervasive Gestalt formation; through the tension of the unfinished situation,  *In Gestalt therapy we try to be consistent with every other event, especially with Nature, because we are a part of Nature.* which is a biological factor. In other words, in Gestalt therapy we try to be consistent with every other event, especially with Nature, because we are a part of Nature.

Source: Bruce Lee's handwritten notes entitled "The Four Basic Philosophical Approaches," contained within his *Misc. Notes* on Gestalt therapy. Bruce Lee Papers.

3-G

THINKING IS REHEARSING

Thinking is rehearsing in fantasy for the role you have to play in society. And when it comes to the moment of performance, and you're not sure whether your performance will be well received, then you get stage fright.

This stage fright has been given by psychiatry the name "anxiety." "What will I have to say on the examination?" "What will I say in my lecture?" You meet a girl and think, "What will I have to wear to impress her?" And so on. All this is rehearsing for the role you play.

In neurosis a part of our personality or of our potential is not available.

"Awareness continuum" "discovering" and "becoming" fully aware of each actual experience. If you can stay with this, you will soon come across some experience that is unpleasant—this critical moment

Thinking is rehearsing in fantasy for the role you have to play in society. And when it comes to the moment of performance, and you're not sure whether your performance will be well received, then you get stage fright.

is the frequent interruption of whatever we experience in the now. This interruption of the awareness continuum prevents maturation, prevents therapy from becoming successful, prevents marriage from becoming richer and deeper, and prevents inner conflicts from being resolved.

The whole purpose of this avoidance tendency is to maintain the status quo (What is the status quo? The status quo is holding on to the concept that we are children). We are infantile because we are afraid to take responsibility in the now. To take our place in history, to be mature, means giving up the concept that we have parents, that we have to be submissive or defiant, or the other variations on the child's role that we play.

Source: Bruce Lee's handwritten notes, untitled, contained within *Misc. Notes.* Bruce Lee Papers.

Artist of Life

MATURATION IS THE DEVELOPMENT FROM ENVIRON-
MENTAL SUPPORT TO SELF-SUPPORT. However the neurotic
child will use his potential, not for self-support but to act out phony
roles. These phony roles are meant to mobilize the environment for
support instead of mobilizing one's own potential. We manipulate
the environment by being helpless, by staying stupid, asking questions, wheedling flattering—the result is that we come to the sticking
point or the impasse.

The impasse occurs when we cannot produce our own support
and when environmental support is not forthcoming. One person
has no eyes, another no ears, another no legs to stand on, another
no perspective, another no emotion. In order to fill these voids, which are usually experienced as boredom with life, emptiness, loneliness, we have to get through the impasse and through the frustrations of the impasse, which usually lead us to shortcut the frustrations and with them the whole learning process.

We manipulate the environment by being helpless, by staying stupid, asking questions, wheedling flattering—the result is that we come to the sticking point or the impasse.

LEARNING

There are two ways of learning. In the first, you get information; you get someone to tell you what concepts will be useful, what the world is like. Then you feed this into your computer and you play the fitting game. Does this concept fit in with these other concepts?

However, the best way of learning is not through the computation of information. Learning is discovering, uncovering what is there in us. When we discover, we are uncovering our own ability, our own eyes, in order to find our potential, to see what is going on, to discover how we can enlarge our lives, to find the means at our disposal that will let us cope with a difficult situation. And all this, I maintain, is taking place in the here and now.

Any speculation about things, any attempt at getting information and assistance from outside help will not produce maturation. So anyone who works with me has to do it with a continuous account of the now. "I am experiencing this; now I feel this; now I don't want to work anymore; now I am bored." From here we can go on to differentiate what of the now experience is acceptable to you, when you want to run away, when you are willing to suffer yourself, when you feel yourself being suffered, and so on. The ability to really see is health and consequently the world is opening up.

Source: Bruce Lee's handwritten notes entitled "Learning," contained within *Misc. Notes. Bruce Lee Papers.*

3-1

THE PROCESS OF "CENTERING"

Centering is the reconciliation of opposites so that they no longer waste energy in useless struggle with each other but can join in "productive combination and interplay."

What is the opposite of existence? The immediate answer would be nonexistence, but this is incorrect. The opposite would be anti-existence, just as the opposite of matter is antimatter. In science we have finally come back to

We in the West think of nothingness as a void, an emptiness, a nonexistence. In Eastern philosophy and modern physical science, nothingness—no-thingness— is a form of process, ever moving.

the pre-Socratic philosopher Heraclitus, who said that everything is flow, flux, process. There are no "things." NOTHINGNESS in Eastern language is "no-thingness." We in the West think of nothingness as a void, an emptiness, a nonexistence. In Eastern philosophy and modern physical science, nothingness—no-thingness—is a form of process, ever moving.

In science we try to find ultimate matter, but the more we split up matter, the more we find other matter. We find movement, and movement equals energy: movement, impact, energy, but no things. Things came about, more or less, by man's need for security. You can manipulate a thing, and you can play fitting games with it. These concepts, these some-things can be put together into something else. "Something" is a thing, so even an abstract noun becomes a thing.

Source: Bruce Lee's handwritten notes entitled "The Process of 'Centering,'" contained within his *Misc. Notes.* Bruce Lee Papers.

PROCESS

To understand the meaning of dealing with things—that in order to bring things back to life, we have to change them into process again. Reification, the making of a thing out of a process, is the functioning of what I call the implosive or catatonic or death layer.

If you have a body, if you have a mind, these things are apparently objects that belong to some instance called "I." "I" am the proud possessor—or the despising possessor—of a mind, of a body, of a world. So in effect I say, "I have some body" (some body) rather than realize that I AM somebody. In Gestalt therapy we look at the way a person manipulates his language, and we see that the more alienated he is from himself, the more he will use nouns instead of verbs, and most especially the word "it."

It is a "thing" that is convenient to use to avoid being alive. When I'm alive, I talk, I am "voicing." When I am dead, I "have" a voice with words; this language will have an expression; and so forth. You notice that this description is mostly a string of nouns, and that all that remains of life is to put them together.

Source: Bruce Lee's handwritten notes entitled "Process," contained within his *Misc. Notes.* Bruce Lee Papers.

3-K

STICKING POINT (IMPASSE—PHOBIC LAYER)

Once we are capable of understanding our reluctance to accept unpleasant experiences, we can get to the next layer, the phobic layer, the resistance, the objection to being what we are. This is where all the should-nots that I have already discussed occur.

If we get behind the phobic state, the objections, we find at that moment the impasse occurs. And within the impasse there is the feeling of being not alive, of deadness. We feel that we are nothing, we are things. In every bit of therapy we have to go through this implosive layer in order to get to the authentic self. This is where most schools of therapy and therapists shrink away, because they also fear deadness. Of course, it is not being dead, but the fear and feeling of being dead, of disappearing. The fantasy is taken for reality.

Once we get through the implosive layer, we see something very peculiar happening. This can be seen most dramatically in the catatonic state, when the patient who

> *In every bit of therapy we have to go through this implosive layer in order to get to the authentic self. This is where most schools of therapy and therapists shrink away, because they also fear deadness.*

has appeared as a corpse explodes to life. And this is what happens when the implosive state is dissolved—explosions happen.

The explosion is the final neurotic layer that occurs when we get through the implosive state. As I see it, this progression is necessary to become authentic. There are essentially four types of explosion: explosion into joy, into grief, into orgasm, into anger. Sometimes the explosions are very mild—it depends on the amount of energy that has been invested in the implosive layer.

Source: Bruce Lee's handwritten notes entitled "Sticking Point (Impasse) (Phobic Layer)" contained within his *Misc. Notes.* Bruce Lee Papers.

The basic phobic attitude is to be afraid to be what you are. And you will find relief immediately if you dare to investigate what you are like. You will find that nothing develops your intelligence better than to take any question and turn it into a genu-

There are essentially four types of explosion: explosion into joy, into grief, into orgasm, into anger. Sometimes the explosions are very mild—it depends on the amount of energy that has been invested in the implosive layer.

ine statement. Suddenly the background will start to open up, and the ground from which the question grows will become visible.

The incredible thing that is so difficult to understand is that experience, awareness of the now, is sufficient to solve all difficulties of this nature, that is, neurotic difficulties. If you are fully aware of the impasse, the impasse will collapse, and you will find yourself suddenly through it (for example, the natural preference of deciding the two items of food).

HESSE ON SELF-WILL

Self-will is the only virtue that takes no account of man-made laws. A self-willed man obeys a different law, the one law I hold absolutely sacred—the law in himself, his own "will."

What does self-willed mean? Does it not mean "having a will of one's own?" The human herd instinct demands adaptation and subordination—but for his highest honor man elects not the meek, the pusillanimous, the supine, but precisely the self-willed man, the heroes.

A self-willed man has no other aim than his own growth. He values only one thing, the mysterious power in himself which bids him live and helps him to grow. The power can be neither preserved nor increased nor deepened by money and power, because money and power are the invention of distrust. Those who distrust the life-giving force within them, or who have none, are driven to compensate through such substitutes as money.

When a man has confidence in himself, when all he wants in the world is to live out his destiny in freedom and purity, he comes to regard all those vastly overestimated and far too costly possessions as mere accessories, pleasant perhaps to have and make use of, but never essential.

His only living destiny is the silent, ungainsayable law in his own heart, which comfortable habits make it so hard to obey but which to the self-willed man is destiny and godhead.

Source: Bruce Lee's handwritten notes entitled "Hesse on Self-Will," contained within his *Misc. Notes.* Bruce Lee Papers.

TOWARD LIBERATION

A choice method is the cultivation of resistance, and where there is resistance there is no understanding. A so-called well-disciplined mind is not a free mind. A choice method, however exacting, fixes the mind in a pattern—a crystallization. Fixing forms can never bring freedom (from fluidity). This type of dead drilling is not an adequate response to the ever-changing moment in combat. This ever-changing moment must be met newly, freshly, for the moment is always new.

Cultivation in classical form is an impediment to truth, for forms are something that has not yet happened. How can a mind which is the result of partialized mechanical form understand the formless?

Cultivation in classical form is an impediment to truth, for forms are something that has not yet happened. How can a mind which is the result of partialized mechanical form understand the formless?

Source: Bruce Lee's handwritten notes entitled "Toward Liberation," contained within his *Misc. Notes.* Bruce Lee Papers.

Part 4

POETRY

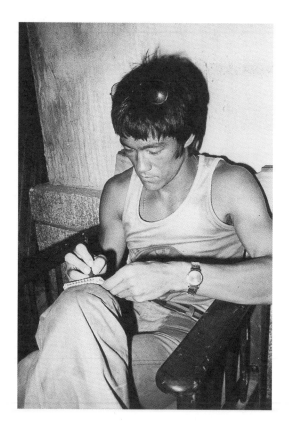

When not working out, writing screenplays, playing with his children or teaching martial art, Lee could often he found writing poetry. He loved the medium as a vehicle through which one's soul could express feelings and sentiments and allow his soul to express itself upon the canvas of life.

Lee also enjoyed translating Chinese poetry into English ("The Frost" we know to be an example of this, originally written in Chinese by the poet Tzu-yeh), and putting his own unique literary interpretation on the original artist's sentiment.

Lee's poems are, by American standards, rather dark—reflecting the deeper, less exposed recesses of the human psyche. Many seem to express a returning sentiment of the fleeting nature of life, love, and the passion of human longing.

Most importantly, these poems reflect another side of Bruce Lee: the sensitive soul, calling out for understanding, love, companionship. His poems reflect his belief that life is what you make it, but the only time available to you for this task is today.

RAIN, BLACK CLOUDS

Rain,
Black clouds,
Fallen blossoms and pale moon,
The hurried flight of birds
The arrival of lonely Autumn
The time for us to part.

The clouds above are floating across the sky
Swiftly, swiftly passing,
Or blending together.

Much has been said, yet we have not
Come to the end of our feelings.
Long must be this parting, and
Remember, remember that all
My thoughts have always been of you.

The good time will probably never come back again.
In a moment—our parting will be over.
When days are short and dull nights long

Read this poem I leave you, read it
When the silence of the world possesses you,
Or when you are fretted with disquiet.
Long must be this parting, and
Remember, remember that all
My thoughts have always been of you.

Source: Bruce Lee's handwritten poem entitled "Rain." Bruce Lee Papers.

4-B

DOWN THE WESTERN HILL

Down the Western Hill the bright sun sinks
Making yellow gold of all the air.

On a lonely hilltop, away from the distant mist,
A golden dragon stands staring, with
Dreams that fade and die in the bright West.

Source: Bruce Lees handwritten poem entitled "Down the Western Hill." Bruce Lee Papers.

THE DYING SUN

The dying sun lies sadly in the far horizon.
The autumn wind blows mercilessly;
The yellow leaves fall.

From the mountain peak,
Two streams parted unwillingly,

One to the West, one to the East.
The sun will rise again in the morning.
The leaves will be green again in spring.
But must we be like the mountain stream,
Never to meet again?

Source: Bruce Lee's handwritten poem entitled "The Dying Sun." Bruce Lee Papers.

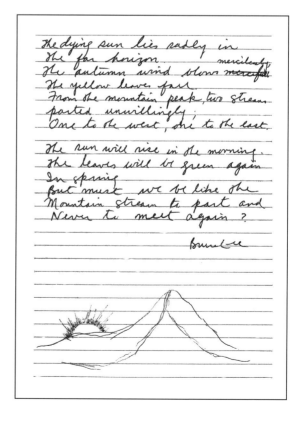

4-D

LOVE IS LIKE A FRIENDSHIP CAUGHT ON FIRE

Love is like a friendship caught on fire.
In the beginning a flame,
Very pretty, often hot and fierce
But still only light and flickering.

As love grows older, our hearts mature
And our love becomes as coals,
Deep-burning and unquenchable.

Source: A poem of Bruce Lee's that he recited to Linda Lee Cadwell, quoted from her book *Bruce Lee: The Man Only I Knew* (New York: Warner Books), © 1975 Linda Lee.

4-E

ONCE MORE I HOLD YOU IN MY ARMS

Once more I hold you in my arms;
And once more I lost myself in
A paradise of my own.

Right now you and I are in
A golden boat drifting freely on a sunny sea
Far, far away from the human world.
I am happy as the waves dancing around us.

Too much analysis kills spontaneity,
As too much light dazzles my eyes.
Too much truth astonishes me.
Despite all obstacles,
Love still exists between us.

It is useless to try to stir the dirt
Out of the muddy water,
As it will become murkier.
But leave it alone,
And if it should be cleared;
It will become clear by itself.

Source: Bruce Lee's handwritten poem, circa 1964. Bruce Lee Papers.

4-F

ALL STREAMS FLOWING EAST OR WEST

All streams flowing East or West
Must flow into the sea;
The current from the middle-
　land
Sweeps by the lonely island.

Gold and silver pebbles mingle,
Seaweed and kelp interlace.
Streams born from mountain
　snows
Grow to swelling wave.

The full-blown arc of quew
　moves
In race against the grey

Caps of white like beats of heart
Are pulled within the wave.

The wave from mountain peaks
　becomes
Hammer to sculpture rocks,
To leave chiseled shapes and
　polished surfaces.
From boulder to rock to sand.
And with the final thrust the sun
Throws wave upon the shore
The jellyfish in weariness
Nestles in a pool.

Source: Bruce Lee's handwritten poem, circa 1963. Bruce Lee Papers.

4-G

BOATING ON LAKE WASHINGTON

I live in memory of a dream
Which has come and gone;
In solitude I sit on my boat
As it glides freely down the tranquil lake.

Across the blue sky, the swallows fly in couples;
On the still water, the Mandarin ducks swim, side by side.
Leaning on the oar I gaze at the water far away.
The sky far away, the loved one far away.

The sun goes down in flame on the far horizon,
And soon the sunset is rushing to its height through
Every possible phase of violence and splendor.
The setting of the sun is supposedly a word of peace,
But an evening like the soft and invisible
Bonds of affection only adds distress to my heart.

Over the lake the round moon rises bright
And floods the horizon with her silver light.
I look into the water; it is as clear as the night.

When the clouds float past the moon,
I see them floating in the lake,
And I feel as though I were rowing in the sky.
Suddenly I thought of you—mirrored in my heart.

The lake sleeps in peace,
Not the faintest murmur of waves can be heard.
Lying back on the boat,
I try to conjure up the land of dream where I may seek for you.
But, alas, no dreams come.
Only a moving point of fire in the dark,
The distant light of a passing boat.

Source: Bruce Lee's handwritten poem entitled "Boating on Lake Washington." Bruce Lee Papers.

FOR A MOMENT

For a moment
The surrounding utters no sound.
Time ceases.
The Paradise of Dreams come true.

Source: Bruce Lee's handwritten poem. Bruce Lee Papers.

4-1

WALKING ALONG THE BANK OF LAKE WASHINGTON

The breeze on the bank
Already blows cool and mild;
The distant merging of lake and sky
Is but a red trace of sunset.

The deep silence of the lake,
Cuts off all tumult from me.
Along the lonely bank
I move with slow footsteps:

Alone the disturbed frogs scurry off.
Here and there are houses,
Cool beads of light spring out from them.

A dazzling moon
Shines down from the lonely depths of the sky.
In the moonlight slowly I move to a gung fu form.
Body and soul are fused into one.

Source: Bruce Lee's handwritten poem entitled "Walking Along the Bank of Lake Washington." Bruce Lee Papers.

4-J

NIGHT RAIN

I sit through the long night
In the high tower,
And listen to the autumn rain
Outside my window.

There is no sound of human life,
Save now and then
A belated traveler hastening by.

Through the dark heaven,
A wild goose wings his lonely flight.
In the chill gloom

A cricket calls
The water drips mournfully
From the t'ung trees;
And the blossoms
Flutter sadly
To the rain-soaked earth.

Sadness broods
Over the world.
I fear to walk in my garden,
Lest I see
A pair of butterflies
Disporting in the sun
Among the flowers.

Source: Bruce Lee's handwritten
poem entitled "Night Rain."
Bruce Lee Papers.

Artist of Life

4-K

OUR TOGETHERNESS IS LIKE A SWEET DREAM

Our togetherness is like a sweet dream
Too sweet, too bitter sweet,
Whose awakening should have been in Paradise.

And now like a dream you will vanish.
And only in dream can we chance to meet again.
That we may live our very lift again,
As July, August, and September.

Dear, do come to me in dreams, that
We may live our very life again
In the land of green.

Much has been said,
Yet I have not come to the end of my feelings.
Driven from my head, you enter my heart.
Remember that my thoughts have always been of you.

When, oh! When shall we walk again.
Hand held in hand
You and I?

Source: Bruce Lee's handwritten poem, untitled, circa 1973. Bruce Lee Papers.

THE SURROUNDINGS UTTER NO SOUND

The surroundings utter no sound.
Time suddenly ceases.
Gently you fall into my arms.

The years of a lifetime never reach a hundred,
Yet they contain a thousand years' sorrow.
When days are short and the dull night long,
Why not take a walk alone in the moonlight?

The bright moon, again, how white it shines,
Shines down on my lonely bed.
For a long time I have stayed in bed with my thoughts,
Racked by sorrow I toss and cannot sleep.
Picking up my clothes, I wander up and down.
The stars and planets are all grown dim in the sky,
Facing the moon, I stand hesitating, alone.
To whom can I tell my sad thought?

The good time will probably never come back again.
In a moment, our parting will be over.
Anxiously, 1 stopped the car by the roadside,
Hesitating, we hold hands.

Source: Bruce Lee's handwritten poem, untitled. Bruce Lee Papers.

The clouds above are floating across the sky,
Swiftly, swiftly passing, or blending together.
Petals fall quietly, birds call in the hills.
From now onwards, long must be our parting,
So let us stop once more for a while.

Like mountain streams, we part and meet again.
Everything is still,
Except the occasional lonely bark of a dog.

4-M

IT IS SPRING

It is spring,
And somewhere in the night
A lute is playing.
It sings of youth and joy,
And love.

But what can it mean to me,
When my heart is with you
A thousand li away?

Source: Bruce Lee's handwritten poem, untitled. Bruce Lee Papers.

Artist of Life

THINGS I SEE

Alone I wander in silence
And in the sky the two escaped parakeets
Fall from fear of fishermen.

The two fish swim;
One white, one gold.
From the picket fence
A pink rose reaches out to the sun.

Among the flowers, two butterflies fly.
They might know where they want to go,
But they do not know how to get there.

Source: Bruce Lee's handwritten poem, untitled. Bruce Lee Papers.

4-0

THE HUMMING BIRD

Rays spring from the East like purple arrows.
The humming bird begins his flight.
Happily he flies through the purple sky,
Looking for the lovely pink rose.

On the mountain peak,
Away from the human world,
He finds the pink rose waiting.
Upon the mountain peak he hovers
In silence above the rose and waits
As dawn from purple grows to gold.

The sun moves on to afternoon,
The time to part.
Unwillingly, the humming bird rises above,
Hovers, circles the rose three times,
Then flies to his nest,
Far, far to the East.

Through my window I have watched
The crimson close of day
Followed by the silver calmness of the night.

In my lonely room no sound stirs.
Who knows that, all evening in bed
I am not sick,
And not even asleep?

Source: Bruce Lee's handwritten poem entitled "The Humming Bird." Bruce Lee Papers.

Artist of Life

A second is an hour,
An hour becomes a night as I lie staring,
Waiting for the sun to rise.
Oh, that I could be a humming bird,
And fly so swiftly to your side.

In dream the most wonderful thing happens
for I am no more a humming bird
and she, no more a pink rose
There is no more noon or night
But always morning.
How I wish that one day
the dream too, is no more a dream.

4-P

THE FROST

Young man,
Seize every minute
Of your time.

The days fly by;
Ere long you too
Will grow old.

If you believe me not,
See there, in the courtyard,
How the frost
Glitters white and cold and
    cruel
On the grass that once was
    green.

Do you not see
That you and I
Are as the branches
Of one tree?

With your rejoicing,
Comes my laughter;
With your sadness
Start my tears.

Love,
Could life be otherwise
With you and me?

Source: A poem entitled "The Frost," by Tzu-yeh, that was translated by Bruce Lee.

4-Q

THE FALLING LEAF

The wind is in high frolic with the rain.
Outside the garden a little yellow leaf
Clinging desperately to its mother branch.

I pick up the leaf
And put it in the book,
Giving it a home.

Source: Bruce Lee's handwritten poem. Bruce Lee Papers.

4-R

THOUGH THE NIGHT WAS MADE FOR LOVING

Though the night was made for loving,
And the day returns too soon.

And so the time flies hopefully
Although she's far away.

Other thoughts may come and go,
But the thought of you,
Remains deeply in my heart.

Source: Bruce Lee's handwritten poem. Bruce Lee Papers.

4-S

THE SILENT FLUTE

I wish neither to possess,
Nor to be possessed.
I no longer covet paradise,
More important, I no longer fear hell.

The medicine for my suffering
I had within me from the very beginning,
But I did not take it.
My ailment came from within myself,
But I did not observe it
Until this moment.

Now I see that I will never find the light
Unless, like the candle, I am my own fuel,
Consuming myself.

Source: "Cord's closing speech," quoted from Bruce Lee's copy of the script of *The Silent Flute,* written by Bruce Lee, dated October 19, 1970. Bruce Lee Papers.

4-T

SINCE YOU LEFT

The sun sets low in the West;
The farewell song is over;
We are separating.

Leaning on the sandalwood oar I gaze at the water,
Far away, the sky.
Far away, the loved one, far away.

Since you left, I know not whether you are far or near,
I only know the colors of nature have paled
And my heart is pent up with infinite yearnings.

Leaning upon the single pillow,
I try to conjure up the Land of Dreams where I may seek for you.
Alas! No dreams come, only the dim lamplight fuses with the shadows.

My boat glides down the tranquil river,
Beyond the orchard which borders the bank.

I leave you my poems.
Read them.

Source: Bruce Lee's handwritten poem, untitled. Bruce Lee Papers.

When the silence of the world possesses you,
Or when you are fretted with disquiet.

In order to go rowing in our boat we have waited
For the setting of the sun.
A slight breeze ripples the blue surface
And stirs the water lilies.

Along the banks,
Where the cherry blossoms fall like rain,
We watch a glimpse of strolling lovers.

Fierce desire pulls me.
I yearn to tell them of passion.
Alas, my boat floats away
At the mercy of the moving current.
My heart looks back in sadness.

Two swallows, and two swallows,
Always the swallows fly in couples.
When they see a tower of jade
Or a lacquered Pavilion,

One never perches there without the other.
When they find a balustrade of marble
Or a gilded window,
They never separate.

Rapidly my boat is gliding down the river,
Under a cloud-strewn sky.
I look into the water;
It is clear as the night.
When the clouds float past the moon,
I see them floating in the river,
And I feel as though I were rowing in the sky.
I think of my beloved
Mirrored so in my heart.

4-U

PARTING

Who knows when meeting shall ever be.
It might be for years or
It might be forever.

Let us then take a lump of clay,
Wet it, pat it,
And make an image of you
And an image of me.
Then smash them, crash them,
And, with a little water,
Knead them together.

And out of the clay we'll remake
An image of you, and an image of me.
Thus in my clay, there's a little of you,
And in your clay, there's a little of me.
And nothing will ever set us apart.

Living, we'll be forever in each other's heart,
And dead, we'll be buried together.

Source: An untitled poem by Madame Kuan, that was translated by Bruce Lee. Madame Kuan was the wife of the great Yuan painter Chao Mengfu and was herself a painter who taught for a time at the Imperial Court. Tradition has it that when in middle age, Chao considered taking a mistress. Madame Kuan wrote her husband this poem, which touched his heart and changed his mind.

Part 5

JEET KUNE DO—THE LIBERATION

Bruce Lee once said of jeet kune do, "It is the art of the soul at peace— like moonlight mirrored in a deep lake."[23] This may sound surprising to some, even to those who were students of Lee at his schools in Oakland, Seattle, and Los Angeles, who recall that the instruction emphasized an efficient and nonclassical approach to combat—as opposed to spiritual truths. Nevertheless, this statement was not merely poetic posturing on Lee's part. Although he was always of a philosophical mind-set, there came a time in Lee's life when all of his prior research into gung fu, philosophy, psychology, and even poetry found expression in the creation of something new—and of a depth seldom seen in the world of martial art.

That something was the formation of a new insight into life that, by extension, influenced Lee's approach to combat. His combative approach was now predicated—for the first time in history—on total freedom for the individual practitioner. Initially, in early 1967, jeet kune do (or JKD, as Lee often referred to it) was a new approach to martial art that was born out of years of scientific research on Lee's part into the human sciences (kinesiology, physiology, and so forth), and it was envisioned by its founder as a simple, direct, and efficient system of all-out combat. However, a back injury Lee sustained (or perhaps, reaggravated) in 1970 forced him to be bed-ridden for a period of several months. Temporarily prevented from being able to train his body, Lee was able to train his mind as never before with the result that he availed himself of deep insights into the human condition which far transcended the purely physical or com-bative realm.

Lee began to find answers. He now began to understand why humans do the things we do—including fighting; our motivations; how we evolve, grow, and develop; and what all of our daily activities ultimately lead to. This caused him to see the limitations inherent in any "system" or "method" of combat—including the highly efficient one he himself had created. Lee began to envision the possibility of a method of "no-method," a "styleless style," that would result in unrestricted athletic and spiritual freedom for the individual practitioner.

Ultimately, then, jeet kune do was not about a more efficient way to subdue one's opponent, but rather it was a more efficient way to subdue oneself; to rid oneself of hang-ups, insecurities, fears, and suppressed emotions—anything, in other words, that would bind the individual from becoming anything less than the fullest expression of himself. Bruce Lee realized that ultimately a person could not obtain the counsel or help he truly required from anybody but himself, leading Lee to write: "Each man must seek out realization himself. No master can give it to him."[24]

What follows in this section are Bruce Lee's commentaries on his new insight into the human condition, beginning with his unique approach to combat for martial artists and ending with a prescription for spiritual freedom for all human beings. Included in this section are eight drafts of an essay that Lee went through in preparing his first public dissertation on his new belief system. The final draft was ultimately published in the September 1971 edition of Black Belt magazine under the title "Liberate Yourself from Classical Karate."[25] (Incidentally, this article was subsequently reprinted in The Legendary Bruce Lee, published by Ohara Publications, Santa Clarita, California, and it is worth reading to witness the final evolution and presentation of his thought process.)

You will find in reading these various drafts that new ideas came to Lee with each writing—all of them significant—and all of them provide us with additional insights and context, further clarifying his views on the ultimate nature of jeet kune do. It is also noteworthy that in his essay entitled "The Ultimate Source of Jeet Kune Do" there is no mention whatsoever about combat—and this, by Lee's own hand—is the ultimate source" of jeet kune do. This marks the first time that all of Lee's essays on jeet kune do have been presented publicly.

5-A

JEET KUNE DO: THE WAY OF THE "STOPPING FIST"

Jeet kune do is training and discipline toward the ultimate reality in combat. The ultimate reality is returning to one's primary freedom, which is simple, direct, and nonclassical.

A good jeet kune do man does not oppose force or give way completely. He is pliable as a spring; he is the complement and not the opposition to his opponent's strength. He has no technique; he makes his opponent's techniques his technique.

One should respond to circumstances without artificial and "wooden" prearrangement. One's action should be like the immediacy of a shadow adapting to a moving object. One's task is simply to complete the other half of the "oneness" spontaneously.

In jeet kune do one does not accumulate but eliminates. It is not daily increase, but daily decrease. The height of cultivation always runs to simplicity. It is the half-way cultivation that runs to ornamentation. So it is not how much fixed knowledge one has accumulated; rather it is what one can apply alively that counts. "Being" is definitely more valued than "doing."

Source: A mimeographed printout that Bruce Lee had given out to members of the LA. Chinatown school, circa 1967.

The understanding of jeet kune do comes through personal feeling from moment to moment in the mirror of relationship and not through a process of isolation. To be is to be related. To isolate is death. Any technique, however worthy and desirable, becomes a disease, when the mind is obsessed with it.

Learn the principles, abide by the principles, and then dissolve the principles. In short, enter a mold without being caged in it, and obey the principles without being bound by them.

My followers in jeet kune do, do listen to this—all fixed

The understanding of jeet kune do comes through personal feeling from moment to moment in the mirror of relationship and not through a process of isolation. To be is to be related. To isolate is death.

set patterns are incapable of adaptability or pliability. The truth is outside of all fixed patterns. Try to obtain the manageable shape of [a] nicely tied paper package of water!

When one has reached maturity in this art, one will have the formless form. It is like the dissolving or thawing [of] ice into water that can shape itself to any structure. When one has no form, one can be all forms; when one has no style, one can fit in with any style.

In primary freedom one uses all ways and is bound by none, and likewise one uses any technique or means that serves one's end. Efficiency is anything that scores.

When you perceive the truth in jeet kune do, you are at the undifferentiated center of a circle that has no circumference.

—Bruce Lee
President of jeet kune do

TOWARD PERSONAL LIBERATION (JEET KUNE DO:I)

In the past many materials were written on, or about jeet kune do, both here and abroad, especially in Hong Kong. However, none of these articles touches its core; it is merely a question of degree of accuracy. Indeed, it is difficult to write about what jeet kune do (JKD) is, though it is easier to write on what it is not.

Maybe to avoid making a THING out of a PROCESS, I have not yet to date written an article on JKD personally. To start this article, a story from Zen seems appropriate:

> A learned man once went to a Zen master to inquire about Zen. As the Zen master talked, the learned man would frequently interrupt him with remarks like, "Oh yes, we have that too," and so forth. Finally the Zen master stopped talking and began to serve tea to the learned man; however, he kept on pouring and the tea cup overflowed. "Enough! No more can go into the cup!" the learned man interrupted. "Indeed, I see," answered the Zen master. "If you do not first empty your cup, how can you taste my cup of tea?"

I hope my comrades in martial art will read the following paragraphs with open-mindedness, leaving all the burdens of preconceived opinions and conclusions behind; this act, by the way, is in itself a liberating power—after all, the usefulness of a cup is in its emptiness.

On the other hand, do relate the material to yourself because although it is on JKD, it is primarily concerned with the blossoming of a martial artist, and not a "Chinese" martial artist, and so forth, and so on. Once and for all let it be noted that a martial artist is first a human being, which is ourselves; nationalities have nothing to do with martial art.

Source: Bruce Lee's handwritten essay entitled "Toward Personal Liberation (Jeet Kune Do)," circa 1971. Bruce Lee Papers.

Artist of Life

*True observation begins when one is devoid of set patterns;
freedom of expression occurs when one is beyond system.*

Supposing several persons who are trained in different forms of combative arts have just witness ed a fight. I am sure we will hear different versions from each of them afterward. The consequence is quite understandable, for one cannot see a fight "as is" because one will "interpret" the fight according to the limits of one's particular conditioning, say from the point of view of a boxer, a wrestler, a karate stylist, a judo-ka, a kung fu man, or anyone who is trained in a particular method. Thus every attempt to describe the fight is really a partial idea of the total fight, depending on one's likes and dislikes. Fighting *as is,* simple and total, is definitely not dictated by your conditioning as a "Chinese" martial artist, a "Korean" martial artist, or "whatever" kind of martial artist you are. True observation begins when one is devoid of set patterns, and freedom of expression occurs when one is beyond systems.

A style is a classified response to one's chosen inclination.

Before we look into JKD let's find out what exactly a classical style of martial art is. To begin with, we must realize the absolute fact that man created style. Disregard the many colorful histories of their founders—by a wise mysterious monk, by special messenger in a dream, in a holy revelation, flooded with golden light, and so forth, and so on. A style should never be the gospel truth, the laws and principles of which can never be violated. Man, the human being, is always more important than any style.

The founder of a style may be exposed to some partial truth, but as time passes by, especially after the founder has passed away, "his" postulates, "his" inclination, "his" concluding formula—we constantly learn, we never conclude—become a law. Creeds are invented, reinforcing ceremonies are prescribed, separative philosophies are formulated, and, finally, the institutions are erected, so what might have started off as some sort of personal fluidity of its founder is now solidified, fixed knowledge—organized and classified response presented in logical order—a preserved cure-all for mass conditioning. In so doing, the well-meaning followers have made this knowledge not only a holy shrine, but a tomb in which the founder's wisdom is buried.

If we honestly look at the reality of combat as it actually is, and not as we would like it to be, I am sure we cannot help but notice that a style tends to bring about adjustment, partiality, denials, condemnation and a lot of justification. In short, the solution being offered is the very cause of the problem, placing limitations and obstacles on our natural growth and consequently obstructing the way to genuine understanding.

Of course, as a direct reaction to "the other truth," another founder or maybe possibly a dissatisfied disciple would "organize" an oppositional approach—as in the case of the soft style versus the hard style, the internal school versus the external school, and so forth—and pretty soon it, too, would become a large organization with its own set laws and its chosen pattern. So begins the

Artist of Life

long struggle with each style claiming to possess the "truth" to the exclusion of all others. So whereas the human being is total and universal—while a style is a partialized projection of an individual and therefore is blinded by that chosen segment and is therefore never the total—the style has long become more important than its practitioners. Worse still is the fact that these styles often are opposed to each other—because they tend to be separated in thoughts from each other; consequently, styles separate men rather than unite them.

Truth cannot be structured or confined.
One cannot express himself fully and totally when a partial set structure or style is imposed upon him. Combat "as is" is total, including all "that is" as well as all "that is not," without favorite lines or angles, having no boundaries, always fresh and alive, [it] is never set and constantly changing. Combat definitely must not be limited to a person's personal inclination, his environmental conditioning, or his physical makeup—although these are parts of the totality of combat. However, it is exactly this kind of "particular security" or "crutch" that limits and blocks the natural growth of a martial artist. In fact, many practitioners develop such a liking for their "crutches" that they can no longer walk without them. Thus any special technique, however classically correct or cleverly designed, is in reality a disease, should one become obsessed with it. Unfortunately, many martial artists are often trapped in such obsessions. These seekers are constantly on the search for that teacher who "satisfies" their particular desires.

What Is Jeet Kune Do?
To set the record straight, I have NOT invented a new style, composite, modified, or otherwise; that is, set within distinct form and laws as apart from "this" style. Jeet kune do is not a form of special conditioning with a set of beliefs and particular approach. It does not look at combat from a certain angle but from all possible angles, and although JKD uses all ways and means to serve its end—after all, efficiency is anything that scores—it is bound by none, and is therefore free from them. In other words, JKD though possessed of all angles, is itself not possessed. For as previously

mentioned, any structure, however efficiently designed, becomes a cage if the practitioner is obsessed with it.

To define JKD as a style—gung fu, karate, kickboxing, Bruce Lee's style of street fighting, and so forth—is to miss the point completely,

Combat definitely must not be limited to a person's personal inclination, his environmental conditioning, or his physical makeup—although these are parts of the totality of combat. However, it is exactly this kind of "particular security" or "crutch" that limits and blocks the natural growth of a martial artist.

because its teaching simply cannot be reduced to a system. If JKD is not a style or a method, some might think it is being neutral or maybe it is indifference. However, this is not the case either, for JKD is both at once "this" and "not this," so it is neither opposed to styles nor not opposed to them. To understand fully, one must... [unfinished].

TOWARD PERSONAL LIBERATION (JEET KUNE DO: II)

I am a teacher as well as a student because I am forever developing and simplifying, but mainly I am known as a teacher, and a notoriously expensive one at that, for when my time is demanded of me my learners pay for its worth.

Time means a lot to me because, you see, I, too, am also a learner and am often lost in the joy of forever developing and simplifying. To interrupt the flow of time to write an article on JKD has not been particularly appealing to me.

In the past many materials were written on or about jeet kune do, both here and abroad, especially in Hong Kong. However, none of these articles touches its core; it is merely a question of degree of accuracy. I am the first to admit [that] to put jeet kune do in a written article is no easy, routine task; indeed, it is difficult to write about what jeet kune do is, although it is definitely easier to write about what it is not.

Not that I care not, but perhaps I wish to avoid making a THING out of a PROCESS, I have not yet to date written an article on JKD. Let me then begin with a Zen story. To some readers this story might be a familiar one; however, I chose it for its appropriateness. Not that Zen is such a mysterious "in" thing or that Zen is anything special. Storytelling is an effective way to limber up the pliability of one's senses, one's attitude and one's mind:

> A learned man once went to a Zen master to inquire about Zen. As the Zen master talked, the learned man would frequently interrupt him with remarks like, "Oh yes, we have that too," and so forth. Finally the Zen master stopped talking and began to serve tea to the learned man; however, he kept on pouring and the tea cup over-flowed. "Enough! No more can go into the cup!" the learned man interrupted. "Indeed, I see," answered the Zen master. "If you do not first empty your cup, how can you taste my cup of tea?"

Source: Bruce Lee's handwritten essay entitled "Toward Personal Liberation (Jeet Kune Do)," circa 1971. Bruce Lee Papers.

My reason tells me it is a vain hope, but I hope those who are steeped in solidified beliefs as well as my comrades in martial art will read the following paragraphs with open-mindedness, leaving all the burdens of preconceived opinions and conclusions behind— this act, by the way, is in itself a liberating process—after all, the usefulness of a cup is in its emptiness.

On the other hand, do relate the material to yourself because although it is on JKD, it is primarily concerned with the blossom-

ing of a martial artist, and not a "Chinese" martial artist, and so forth, and so on. A martial artist is first a human being, which we are ourselves; nationalities have nothing to do with martial art. To live is a constant process of relating, so please cease all that mental chattering, come on out of that protective shell of isolation, that proud conclusion, or whatever, and relate DIRECTLY to what is being said. Cease all that intellectual or mental mumble jumble and return to your senses, and bear in mind I seek neither your approval nor to influence you. Instead of making up your mind and saying, "So this is this," and "That is that," I will be more than satisfied if as a result of this article you begin to learn to investigate everything yourself from now on.

True Observation Begins When One is Devoid of Set Patterns; Freedom of Expression Occurs When One is Beyond System.

Supposing several persons who are trained in different forms of combative arts have just witnessed a fight. I am sure we will hear different versions from each of them afterwards. The consequence is quite understandable, for one cannot see a fight "as is," say from the points of view of a boxer, a wrestler, a karate stylist, a judo-ka, a kung fu man, or anyone who is trained in a particular method, because he is so often blinded by his chosen segments and naturally will "interpret" the fight according to the limits of his particular conditioning.

Thus every attempt to describe the fight is really a partialized idea of the totality of the fight, depending on one's likes and dislikes. Fighting as is, simple and total, is definitely not dictated by your conditioning as a "Chinese" martial artist, a "Korean" martial artist, or "whatever" kind of martial artist. True observation begins when one is devoid of set patterns, and freedom of expression occurs when one is beyond systems.

A *Style is a Classified Response to One's Chosen Inclination.*
Before we look into JKD, let's find out what exactly is a classical style of martial art. To begin with, we must realize the absolute fact that man created style. Disregard the many colorful origins of their founders—by a wise mysterious hermit monk, by a special messenger in a dream, in a holy revelation, and so forth, and so on. A style should never be the gospel truth, the laws and principles of which can never be violated. Man, the live, creative human being, is always more important than any established, sterile style.

Let's say the founder of a style was exposed to some partial truth, and even if in this process of discovery he had not attempted to organize this partial truth, after he died "his" postulates, "his" inclination, and, very possibly, "his" concluding formula— we constantly learn, my friends; we never conclude—were turned into a law by his students and followers. Creeds were invented, solemn reinforcing ceremonies were prescribed, separative philosophies were formulated, and, finally, institutions were erected so that what might have started off as some sort of personal fluidity of its founder has now become solidified, fixed knowledge—an organized and classified response presented in logical order—a preserved cure-all for mass conditioning.

In so doing, the well-meaning, loyal followers have made this knowledge not only a holy shrine, but a tomb in which the founder's wisdom is buried. Of course, as a natural reaction to "the other truth," another founder or maybe possibly a dissatisfied disciple would "organize" an oppositional approach—as in the case of the soft style versus the hard style, the internal school versus the external school, and so forth—and pretty soon, it too would become a large organization with its own set laws and its chosen pattern. So begins the long struggle with each style claiming to possess the "truth" to the exclusion of all others. Styles are merely partialized and organized parts of a unitary whole.

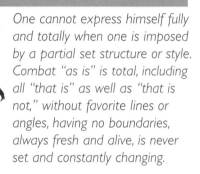

One cannot express himself fully and totally when one is imposed by a partial set structure or style. Combat "as is" is total, including all "that is" as well as "that is not," without favorite lines or angles, having no boundaries, always fresh and alive, is never set and constantly changing.

If we honestly look at the reality of combat as it actually is, and not as we would like it to be, I am sure we cannot help but notice that a style tends to bring about adjustment, partiality, denials, condemnation, and a lot of justification. In short, the solution being offered is the very cause of the problem, placing limitations and obstacles on our natural growth and consequently obstructing the way to genuine understanding.

The sad fact is that because styles tend to be separated in thought from each other, and consequently opposed to each other, styles keep men apart from each other rather than uniting them.

Truth Cannot Be Structured or Confined.

One cannot express himself fully and totally when one is imposed by a partial set structure or style. Combat "as is" is total, including all "that is" as well as "that is not," without favorite lines or angles, having no boundaries, always fresh and alive, is never set and constantly changing. Combat definitely must not be limited to your personal inclination, your environmental conditioning, or your physical makeup—although these are parts of the totality of combat. However, it is exactly this kind of "particular security" or "crutch" that limits and blocks the total natural growth of a martial artist. In fact, many of these practitioners develop such a liking for his "crutches" that he can no longer walk without them. Thus any special technique, however classically correct or cleverly designed, is in reality a disease, should one become obsessed with it.

Unfortunately, many martial artist seekers, past or present, are often trapped in such obsessions. They are constantly on the search for that teacher who "satisfies" their particular diseases.

What is Jeet Kune Do?

Or more appropriately, what jeet kune do is not. Once and for all let it be known that I have NOT invented a new style, composite, modified or otherwise; that is, set within distinct form and laws as apart from "this" style.

JKD is not a form of special conditioning with a set of beliefs and particular approach. It does not look at combat from a certain angle but from all possible angles, and although jeet kune do utilizes all ways and means to serve its end—after all, efficiency is anything that scores—it is bound by none, and is therefore free from them. In other words, JKD, though possessed of all angles, is itself not possessed. For any obsession with any structure, however efficiently designed, can easily become a cage: Be aware!

To define JKD as a style—gung fu, karate, kickboxing, Bruce Lee's style of street fighting, and so forth—is to miss its intention completely, for its teaching simply cannot be reduced to a system. If JKD is not a style or a method, some might think it is being neutral or maybe it is indifference. However, this is not the case either, for JKD is both at once "this" and "not this," so naturally it is neither opposed to styles nor not opposed to them. To understand this fully, one must... [unfinished].

JEET KUNE DO: WHAT IT IS NOT (JEET KUNE DO: III)

In the past, quite a few articles were written on or about jeet kune do (JKD), both here and in Hong Kong. However, none of these articles touches its core; it is merely a question of degree of accuracy.

I am the first to admit that any attempt to crystallize jeet kune do into a written article is no easy, routine task. Indeed, it is difficult to write about what jeet kune do is, although it is a bit easier to write on what it is not. Perhaps to avoid making a thing out of a process, I have not yet to date written an article on JKD.

Let me then begin with a Zen story. To some readers, this story might well be a familiar one. I have chosen this story for its appropriateness—not that Zen is such a mysterious "in" thing or that Zen is anything special, which it is not. Look upon this story as a sort of limbering up for the pliability of one's senses, one's attitude, and one's mind. You need that to read this article; otherwise you might as well forget about it.

> A learned man once went to a Zen teacher to inquire about Zen. As the Zen teacher explained, the learned man would frequently interrupt him with remarks like, "Oh, yes, we have that, too...." Finally, the Zen teacher stopped talking and began to serve tea to the learned man. However, he kept on pouring, and the tea cup over-flowed. "Enough!" the learned man once more interrupted. "No more can go into the cup!" "Indeed, I see," answered the Zen teacher. "If you do not first empty your cup, how can you taste my cup of tea?"

Source: Bruce Lee's handwritten essay entitled "Jeet Kune Do: What It Is Not," circa 1971. Bruce Lee Papers.

I hope my comrades in martial art will read the following paragraphs with open-mindedness, leaving all the burdens of preconceived opinions and conclusions behind. This act, by the way, has in itself a liberating power. After all, the usefulness of a cup is in its emptiness.

On the other hand, do relate this article to yourself because although it is on JKD, it is primarily concerned with the blossoming of a martial artist—not a "Chinese" martial artist, a "Japanese" martial artist, and so forth. A martial artist is first a human being, which we are ourselves; nationalities have nothing to do with martial arts. So please come out of that protective shell of isolation, that proud conclusion or whatever, and relate directly to what is being said—once again return to your senses by ceasing all that intellectual or mental mumbo jumbo.

Remember well that living is a constant process of relating. Remember, too, that I seek neither your approval nor to influence you to my way of thinking. I will be more than satisfied if, as a result of this article, instead of making up your mind and saying, "So this is this," and "That is that," you learn to investigate everything for yourself from now on.

On Choiceless Observation

Supposing several persons who are trained in different styles of combative arts have just witnessed an all-out street fight. I am sure we will hear different versions from each of these stylists afterwards. The consequence is quite understandable, for a person cannot see a fight "as is"—because he is so often blinded by his chosen segments from the point of view of a kung fu stylist, a boxer, a karate man, a wrestler, a judoka, or anyone who is trained in a particular method, and naturally he will interpret the fight according to the limits of his particular conditioning. Fighting as is—simple and total—is definitely not dictated by your conditioning as a "Chinese" martial artist, a "Korean" martial artist, or "whatever" type of martial artist you are. True observation begins when one is devoid of favorite set patterns, and freedom of expression occurs when one is beyond systems.

A style is a classified response to one's chosen inclination.

Before we look into JKD, let's find out what exactly is a classical style or martial art. To begin with, we must realize the absolute fact that man created styles. Disregard the many colorful origins of their founders—by a wise, mysterious monk, by special messenger in a dream, in a holy revelation, and so forth. A style should never be the gospel truth, the laws and principles of which can never be violated. Man, the live, creative human being, is always more important than any established, set style.

Let's say a long time ago a martial artist was exposed to some partial truth. Even if in his process of discovery he had not attempted to organize this partial truth, which has been such a common tendency in man's search for security and certainty in life, after he died, "his" hypothesis, "his" partial inclination, "his" postulates, and, most likely, "his" concluding formula (we constantly learn, we never conclude) would be turned into a law by his students and followers. Impressive creeds would be invented, solemn reinforcing ceremonies prescribed, separative philosophy and patterns would be formulated, and so forth, and so on, and finally an institution would be erected. So what might have started off as some sort of personal fluidity on the part of its founder has now become solidified, fixed knowledge— organized and classified responses presented in logical order—a sort of preserved cure-all for mass conditioning. In so doing, the well-meaning, loyal followers have made this knowledge not only a holy shrine, but a tomb in which the founder's wisdom is buried.

Of course, as a natural reaction to "the other's truth," another martial artist, or possibly a dissatisfied disciple, would organize an oppositional approach, as in the case of the soft style versus the hard style, the internal school versus the external school, and all these separative nonsenses. Pretty soon, this approach, too, would become a large organization with its own set laws and chosen pattern. So the long rivalry has begun, with each style claiming to possess the truth to the exclusion of all the others; whereas at best styles are merely parts dissected from a unitary whole.

If we honestly look at the reality of combat as it actually is, and not as we would like it to be, I am sure we cannot help but notice that a style tends to bring about adjustment, partiality, denials, condemnation, and a lot of justification. In short, the solution being offered is the very cause of the problem, placing limitation and obstacles on our natural growth and obstructing the way to genuine understanding. Because they are often separated in thoughts from each other and, consequently, opposed to each other, styles keep men apart from each other rather than uniting them.

Truth cannot be structured or confined.
A person cannot express himself fully and totally when a partial set structure or style is imposed upon him. Combat "as is" is total, including all "that is" as well as all "that is not," without favorite lines or angles, having no boundaries, always fresh and alive; it is never set and is constantly changing. Martial art definitely must not be limited to your personal inclination, your environmental conditioning, or your physical makeup, although these are also parts of the totality of martial art.

Should there be confinement of any sort—that is, setting combat into a chosen mold—there will always be a resistance between one's set pattern of "what should be" as opposed to the ever-changing "what is." It pays to remember that the whole is evidenced in all parts, but an isolated part, efficient or not, does not constitute the whole. So one might say "a little learning is a

Artist of Life

dangerous thing" applies appropriately to those who are conditioned to a particular approach to combat.

Maybe because a person does not want to be left uncertain or insecure, he organizes a choice pattern of combat. No matter what the reason is, followers are being enclosed and controlled within a style's limitation, which is certainly less than their own human potential. Like anything else, prolonged imitative drilling will certainly promote mechanical precision and habitual routine security. However, it is exactly this kind of "particular security" or "crutch" that limits and blocks the total growth of a martial artist. In fact, quite a few practitioners develop such a liking for their "crutches" that they can no longer walk without them. Thus any special technique, however cleverly designed, is actually a disease, should one become obsessed with it. Unfortunately, many martial art seekers, past and present, are often trapped in such obsessions. They are constantly on the search for that teacher who "satisfies" their particular diseases.

What Jeet Kune Do Is Not
Once and for all let it be known that I have not invented a new style—composite, modified, or otherwise; that is, a style set within distinct form and laws as apart from "this" style or "that" method.

On the contrary, I hope to free my comrades from clinging to styles, patterns, or doctrines.

What, then, exactly is jeet kune do? Literally, *jeet* means "to intercept, to stop"; *kune*, "fist"; *do*, "the way, the ultimate reality"—or, "the way of the intercepting fist." Remember that the term *jeet kune do* is merely a name used, a mirror in which we see ourselves. I am neither interested nor concerned with the term; I am more interested in its liberating factor.

Unlike the traditional approach, there is never a series of rules, a classification of techniques, and so forth, and so on, that constitutes a so-called JKD method of fighting. To begin with, there is no such thing as a method of fighting. To create such a method is pretty much like putting a pound of water into wrapping paper and shaping it, although many futile arguments exist today as to the choice of colors, textures, and so forth, and so on, of the wrapping paper.

Briefly, then, JKD is not a form of special conditioning with a set of beliefs and particular approach. It does not look at combat from a certain angle but from all possible angles, and although JKD utilizes all ways and means to serve its end (after all, efficiency is anything that scores), it is bound by none and is, therefore, free

Artist of Life

from all ways and means. In other words, JKD, though possessed of all angles, is itself not possessed, to be in it but not of it.

To define JKD as a style (gung fu, karate, kickboxing, Bruce Lee's style of street fighting, and so forth, and so on) is to miss the point completely, for its teaching simply cannot be reduced to a system. If JKD is not a style or a method, some might think it is neutral or maybe it is indifferent. However, this is not the case either, for JKD is both at once "this" and "not this." So naturally it is neither opposed to styles nor not opposed to them. To understand this fully, one must transcend the duality of "for" and "against" and look at one organic whole. Within the absolute there is simply no distinction; everything is. A good JKD man rests in direct intuition.

Oftentimes, the question is asked whether JKD is against form. It is true that there is no prearranged sets or *kata* in the teaching of JKD. However, we know, through instinctive body feel, that in any physical movement and for each individual there is always a most efficient and alive manner to accomplish the purpose of the performance, that is, with regard to proper leverage, balance in motion, economical and efficient use of motion and energy, and so forth, and so on. Live, efficient movements that liberate are one thing. Sterile, classical sets that bind and condition are another. Also, there is a subtle difference between "having no form" and having "no-form." The first is ignorance, the second, transcendence.

Art is the freedom of expression of the self.
If mere mechanical routine efficiency will make everyone a martial artist, then all is well. Unfortunately, combat, like freedom, is something that cannot be preconceived. Preformations simply lack the flexibility and totality to adapt to the ever changing.

At this point, many would ask, "How, then, do we gain this unlimited freedom?" I cannot tell you because it will then become an approach. Although I can tell you what is not, I cannot tell you what is. That, my friend, you will have to find out all by yourself, for it is time to awaken to a simple fact, and that is that there is no help but self-help. What is more, who says we have to "gain" freedom?

Being wise in traditional martial art seems to be a constant process of accumulating fixed knowledge; like a first degree knows so many sets or techniques, a second degree a little more; or an "X" brand martial artist, a kicker, should accumulate "Y" brand's hand technique, or vice versa.

We do not have to "gain" freedom because freedom has always been with us and is not something to be gained in the end through strict and faithful adherence to some definite formulas. Formulas can only inhibit freedom and preformations only squelch creativity and impose mediocrity. So-called spiritual training promotes not the promised internal power but psychological constipation. Bear in mind that freedom is not an ideal, an end to be desired. We do not "become"; we simply "are." The training in martial art is toward this: "being" mind, rather than "having" mind, liberating the spirit rather than binding the body.

Learning is definitely not mere imitation or the ability to accumulate and conform to fixed knowledge. Learning is a constant process of discovery and never a concluding one. In JKD we begin not by accumulation but by discovering the cause of our ignorance, and oftentimes this involves a shedding process. Patterns, techniques, doctrines, and so forth, and so on, touch only the fringe of genuine understanding. Its core, however, lies in the individual mind, and until that is touched, everything is still uncertain and only superficial. Truth will not come until we have come to understand personally the whole process of the working of our being. After all, ultimately, knowledge in martial art simply means self-knowledge, and JKD can become intelligible only in the vigorous and constant process of self-inquiry and self-discovery.

Unfortunately, most of the students in martial art are conformers. The student seldom learns to depend upon himself for expression. Instead, he faithfully or blindly follows an instructor, the authority figure, and his instructor's imposed pattern. That way, the student feels he is no longer alone and finds security in mass imitation. However, what is nurtured is the dependent mind rather than independent inquiry, which is so essential to genuine understanding. So through daily conditioning a student will probably be skillful according to a pattern; however, he will not come to understand himself.

Most martial art teachers are fixed in a routine. Because they depend on a method and merely drill systematic routines, they can only produce patternized prisoners according to a lifeless, systematizing concept. A teacher, a really good teacher, is never a giver of truth; he is a guide, a pointer to truth.

Therefore, a good teacher, or, more appropriately, a guide, studies each student individually and helps to awaken the student to explore himself, both internally and externally, and ultimately to integrate himself with his being. For example, to assist his student's growth, a teacher might confront the student with skillful frustrations. All in all, a teacher acts as a catalyst, and not only must he have a tremendous understanding; he must also possess a sensitive mind with great flexibility and adaptability.

To change with change is the changeless state.

How often we are told by different "professors" and "masters"— and we do have many philosophers and desk researchers around— that martial art is life itself? I wonder how many of them really understand. To be sure, life does not mean stagnation, a partialized something or a confining frame. Life is a constant movement, rhythmic as well as un-rhythmic movement. Also life is a constant changing process.

Instead of flowing with this process of change choicelessly, many of the martial art "masters," past and present, have built an illusion of fixed forms, solidifying the ever flowing, dissecting the totality, organizing chosen pattern, planning spontaneity, and so forth, and so on. Look around and you will find in martial art now we have an assortment of routine performers, trick artists, insensitized patternized robots, glorifiers of the past—all organizers of despair.

The pitiful sight is to see the sincere students earnestly repeating those imitative drills, listening to their own screams and spiritual yells. In most cases, the means being offered are so elaborate that tremendous attention must be given to them, and gradually the end is forgotten. So what these students are doing is merely performing their methodical routines as response rather than responding to "what is." They no longer "listen" to circumstances; they "recite" their circumstances. These poor souls have unknowingly become a classical mess. They are the "product" of conditioning that was prescribed for them hundreds and thousands of years ago.

A Finger Pointing to the Moon

There is no standard in total combat, and expression must be free. That liberating truth is a reality only insofar as it is experienced and lived in its suchness by the individual himself, and this truth is far beyond any styles or disciplines. Remember, too, that JKD is just a term used, a boat to get one across, and once across it is to be discarded and not carried on one's back. These few paragraphs at best are merely "a finger pointing to the moon." Please do not take the finger to be the moon or fix your intense gaze on the finger and thus miss the beautiful sight of heaven. After all, the usefulness of the finger is in pointing away from itself to the light that illumines finger and all.

5-E

TOWARD PERSONAL LIBERATION (JEET KUNE DO: IV)

The usefulness of the cup is in its emptiness.

A learned man once went to a Zen teacher to inquire about Zen. As the Zen teacher explained, the learned man would frequently interrupt him with remarks like, "Oh, yes, we have that, too..." Finally, the Zen teacher stopped talking and began to serve tea to the learned man. However, he kept on pouring, and the tea cup over-flowed. "Enough!" the learned man once more interrupted. "No more can go into the cup!" "Indeed, I see," answered the Zen teacher. "If you do not first empty your cup, how can you taste my cup of tea?"

I hope my comrades will read the following paragraphs with open-mindedness, leaving all the burdens of preconceived opinions and conclusions behind—this act, by the way, has in itself a liberating power—on the other hand, do relate this article to your

Source: Bruce Lee's handwritten essay entitled "Toward Personal Liberation fleet Kune Do)," circa 1971. Bruce Lee Papers.

self because although it is about JKD, it is primarily concerned with the blossoming of a martial artist—and not a "Chinese" martial artist, a "Japanese" martial artist, and so forth, and so on. A martial artist is first a man, which we are ourselves; nationalities have nothing to do with martial art. I am asking you not to accept nor to deny what is said; all I ask is that you suspend judgment and listen choicelessly.

Supposing several persons who are trained in different combative arts have just witnessed a fight. I am sure we will hear different versions of it afterwards. The consequence is quite understandable, for one cannot see a fight "as is" because he will see the fight according to the limits of his particular conditioning—say from the point of views of a boxer, a wrestler, a karateka, a judoka, a gung fu man, or anyone who is trained in a particular method. Every attempt to describe the fight is really an intellectual and emotional reaction, a partial idea of the total fight; in this case, the reaction depends on one's likes and dislikes. Fighting is not something dictated by your conditioning as a Korean martial artist, a Chinese martial artist, and so forth, and so on. True observation begins when one is devoid of favorite set patterns, and freedom of expression occurs when one is beyond systems.

Style

Just what is a classical style of martial art? First and foremost, we must realize the fact that man created styles. Disregard the many fancy historical origins of their founders—by a wise ancient monk, by special messenger in a dream, in a holy revelation, and so forth—a style should never be the gospel truth, the laws and principles of which can never be violated. Man, the human being, is always more important than any style.

The founder of a style might be exposed to some partial truth, but as time passed by, especially after the founder passed away, this partial truth became a law, or worse still, a prejudiced faith against the "different" styles. In order to pass along this knowledge from generation to generation, the various responses had to be organized and classified, and present in logical order. Creeds were invented, reinforcing ceremonies were set to glorify, separative philosophies established and organizations erected. So a definite

Artist of Life

form resulted and all those who come to learn will be bound by that form.

So what might have started off as some sort of personal fluidity on the part of its founder is now solidified knowledge, a sort of preserved cure-all for mass conditioning. In the process the faithful followers have made this knowledge not only a holy shrine, but a tomb in which the founder's wisdom is buried. Because of the nature of organization and preservation, the means become so elaborated that tremendous attention must be devoted to them, and gradually the end is forgotten.

If we honestly look at reality as it is, and not as we would like [it] to be, I am sure we cannot help but notice that a style tends to bring about partiality, adjustments, interpretation, justification, condemnation, denials, and so on; in short, the solution being offered is the very cause of the problem, placing obstacles and limitations in the light that will illumine our shadows [and impeding our] way to understanding. If we really and totally see organically, then we find that the end is also in the means, the answer is in the question, each being the cause as well as the result of each other.

At any rate, the followers of a combat style often accept its "organized segment" as the total reality of combat. Of course, as a direct reaction to "the other truth," another founder or maybe a dissatisfied disciple might "organize" an oppositional approach, and pretty soon it, too, would become a large organization with its own laws and fixed fragmentary patterns. These styles arise from the division of a unitary total, and not only do they tend to be separated in thoughts from each other, and consequently opposing each other— thus keeping people apart—but each style also claims to posses "truth" to the exclusion of all the others. So whereas the individual is total and universal—while a particular style is partialized, blinded by that chosen segment and therefore is never the total—the style has long become more important than its practitioners.

Style: "It is a classified response to one's chosen inclination."
A person cannot express himself fully and totally when a partial set structure or style is imposed upon him. Combat "as is" is total (including all "that is" as well as all "that is not"), without favorite

lines or angles, having no boundaries and always fresh and alive; is never set and constantly changing. Combat definitely must not be limited to your personal inclination, your physical makeup, or your environmental conditioning—although these are also parts of the total combat. Should there be any confinement of any sort, that is, setting combat into a choice mold; there will always be a resistance of your set pattern of "what should be" as opposed to the ever-changing "what is."

Remember that the whole is evidenced in all the parts, but an isolated part, efficient or not, does not constitute the whole. In the field of law, there are criminal lawyers, business lawyers, and so forth; unfortunately, no such thing occurs in "all-in/total fighting." Favorite segments do not fare too well in "all-in/total fighting." So one can say "a little learning is a dangerous thing" applies appropriately to those who are conditioned to a particular approach to combat.

Once we see that a style has the tendency to "set" and "trap" reality into a chosen mold, we will then understand that this professed cure is itself a disease. Maybe because people do not want to be left uncertain or insecure, they "organize" a choice pattern of combat. Disregard the cause, its followers are being "enclosed" and "controlled" within the style's limitation, which is certain-

Artist of Life

ly less than their own potential. Like anything else, prolonged imitative drilling will certainly promote mechanical precision and a habitual pattern of security; however, it is this kind of "particular security" or "crutch" that limits and blocks the natural growth and hinders a martial artist in his journey to his reunion with his total being. Many martial artists develop such a liking for their "crutches" that they can no longer walk without them. Thus any special technique, however classically correct or cleverly designed, is a disease, should one become obsessed with it. Many martial artists, ranked or un-ranked, are often trapped in such obsessions. These martial artists, not unlike most of the martial art seekers, are constantly on the search for that teacher who "satisfies" their particular diseases.

What Is JKD?

To set the record straight, I have NOT invented a new style, composite, modified or otherwise, that is, a style or method set within distinct form and laws as apart from "this" style or "that" method. On the contrary, I hope to free my followers from clinging to styles, patterns, or molds. More about this later, but in the meantime, do remember that the term *jeet kune do* is merely a name used, a mirror in which we see ourselves. The brand name is really nothing special.

Unlike the traditional approach, there is not a series of rules, a classification of techniques, and so forth, that constitute a so-called JKD method of fighting. To begin with, let me be the first to tell you that there is no such thing as a method of fighting. To create such a method is pretty much like putting a pound of water into wrapping paper and shaping it—although [many] futile arguments exist nowadays as to the choice of colors, textures, and so forth, of the wrapping paper.

Briefly, JKD is not a form of specialized conditioning with a set of beliefs and a particular approach. So basically it is not a "mass" art. Structurally, it does not look at combat from a certain angle but from all possible angles, because it is not bound to any system. And, consequently, its techniques cannot be reduced to a system. And although it utilizes all ways and means to serve its end (efficiency is anything that scores), it is bound by none, and it is therefore free from all ways and means. In other words, JKD, although possessed of all angles, is itself not possessed; for as previously mentioned, any structure, however efficiently designed, becomes a cage if the practitioner is obsessed with it. To define JKD as a style (gung fu, karate, kickboxing, and so forth) is to miss the point completely, for its teaching cannot be reduced to a system. If JKD is not a style or a method, maybe it is neutral or maybe it is indifferent. However, this is not the case either, for JKD is both at once "this" and "not this," and JKD is neither opposed to styles nor not opposed to them. To understand fully, one must transc end the duality of "for" and "against" and look at one organic whole. Within the totality there is simply no distinction; everything IS. A good JKD artist rests in direct intuition.

"Having No Form" and Having "No-Form"
Oftentimes the question is asked whether JKD is against form. It is true that there are no prearranged sets or kata in the teaching of JKD; however, we know, through body-feel, that in any physical movement there is always a most efficient and alive manner for each individual to accomplish the purpose of the performance—

that is, with regard to proper leverage, balance in motion, economical and efficient use of motions and energy, and so on. Live, efficient movement that liberates is one thing; sterile, classical sets that bind and condition are another. Also, there is a subtle difference between "having no form" and having "no-form"; the first is ignorance, the second, transcendence.

If mere mechanical routine efficiency will make everyone a martial artist, then all is well; unfortunately, combat, like freedom, is something that cannot be preconceived. Preformations simply lack the flexibility to adapt to the ever changing. At this point, many would ask how, then, do we gain this unlimited freedom? I cannot tell you because it will then become an approach. Although I can tell you what is not, I cannot tell you what is. "That," my friend, you will have to find out all by yourself, for it is time to awaken to a simple truth, and that is: there is no help but self-help. What is more, who says we have to "gain" freedom?

In traditional martial art being wise seems to be a constant process of accumulating of fixed knowledge—like a first degree knows so many sets or techniques, a second degree a little more; or an X brand martial artist, a kicker, should accumulate Y brand's hand techniques, or vice versa. Accumulating fixed knowledge of oneself externally is not the process of JKD; rather, JKD is a process of discovering the cause of one's ignorance, and oftentimes involves a shedding process. Accumulating fixed knowledge does not necessarily bring about truth. Truth comes to us when we understand personally the whole process of working on our being. No amount of fixed knowledge or "secret teaching" can be compared to clarity of understanding. Patterns, doctrines, and so forth, touch only the fringe of martial art. Its core lies in the human mind, and, until that is touched, everything is still superficial and uncertain.

Remember, my comrades, that ultimately, knowledge in martial art simply means self-knowledge, and JKD can become intelligible only in the vigorous and constant process of self-discovery. Previously I have said that we do not have to "gain" freedom because freedom has always been with us, and it [is] not something to be gained at the end through strict adherence to some particular formulas. Freedom is not an ideal, an end to be desired. We do not "become," we simply "are." Therefore, training in JKD is toward this: "being" mind, rather than "having" mind. Once and for all, do come to the realization that sterile patterns are incapable of such liveliness and freshness, and preformations only squelch creativity and impose mediocrity. Also, the mystical mind training promotes not the promised internal power, but psychological constipation. In JKD, whether it is inward or outward training, the techniques used are oftentimes temporary expedients, the aims of which are to liberate the spirit rather than to bind the body.

When I first arrived in the United States I was teaching my own version of the wing chun style—I had my "Chinese" system then. However, since then I am no longer interested in systems or organization. Organized institutes tend to produce patternized prisoners of a systematized concept, and the instructors are often fixed in a routine. Of course, what is worse is that, by imposing a lifeless preformation, their natural growth is blocked.

A teacher, a really good teacher, functions as a pointer to truth, but not a giver of truth. He employs a minimum of form to lead his student to the formless. Furthermore, he points out the importance of being able to enter a mold but not being caged in it, or to follow the principles without being bound by them. For a pliable, choiceless observation without exclusion is so essential in the cultivation of martial art—an "altogether alert awareness" without its center or its circumference, to be in it, but not of it. Above all, a teacher should not depend on a method and drill systematic routines; instead, he studies each individual student and awakens him to explore himself, both internally and externally, and ultimately to integrate himself with his being. Such teaching, which is really no teaching, requires a sensitive mind with great flexibility and adaptability, and it is difficult to come by nowadays.

Sincere and serious learners are equally difficult to come by, too. Many students are five-minute enthusiasts; some of them come in with selfish motives, but unfortunately, most of them are second hand artists, basically conformers. An average practitioner in the martial art seldom learns to express himself; instead, he faithfully follows an instructor, the authority figure, and an imposed pattern. I guess a person finds more security in mass imitation; unfortunately what is nurtured is the depending mind rather than independent inquiry. These tradition-bound teachers

Artist of Life

reinforce the conditioning through their daily teaching and will not try to understand reality as it is because it condemns them. As time goes by their practitioners might understand some routines and might even become skillful according to a particular pattern. However, they have not come to understand themselves. In other words, they have gained control of the manipulative routine skill they have, but not what they are in themselves.

Martial art is not merely the physical act of filling time and space through some sort of precision-like movement. Machines can do that, too. As he matures, a martial artist will realize that his kick or punch is really not so much a tool for conquering his opponent, but a tool to explode through his consciousness, his ego, his fear, and all his mental blocks. Indeed, the kicks and punches are ultimately means for penetrating the depth of his being so that he can restore the equilibrium of his inner center of gravity and achieve harmony. With this vital inward loosening flows his outward expression of his tools. Behind each movement of an accomplished martial artist is this wholeness of being, this all-inclusive attitude.

As he matures, a martial artist will realize that his kick or punch is really not so much a tool for conquering his opponent, but a tool to explode through his consciousness, his ego, his fear, and all his mental blocks.

How often we are told by different "masters" and "professors"—and we do have many abstract philosophers and desk researchers around—that martial art is life itself; however, I wonder how many of them really appreciate that statement and truly understand. To be sure, life is not a partialized something, a frame. Life is never stagnation. It is a constant movement, unrhythmic movement, as well as constant change. Instead of flowing with this change choicelessly, many of the martial art "masters," past and present, have built an illusion of fixed forms, solidifying the ever flowing, dissecting the totality, organizing chosen patterns, planning spontaneity, separating the harmonious unity into the duality of the soft versus the firm, indulging in creation and glorification of the "good old times," and so forth, and so on.

The result is quite evident. In martial art we have an assortment of routine performers, trick artists, cream puffs, organized despair, and many insensitized patternized robots around listening to their own screams and spiritual yells. They are merely performing their methodical routines as responses rather than responding to "what is." They no longer "listen" to circumstances; they "recite their circumstances." These poor soulsin martial art have become those organized forms; they are those classical blocks. In short, they are the "product" of conditioning that has been handed down for hundreds and thousands of years.

There is no standard in total combat, and expression must be free. That liberating truth is a reality only insofar as it is experienced and lived in its suchness by the individual himself, and this truth is far beyond any styles or disciplines. Remember, too, that JKD is just a name used, a boat to get one across, and once across [it] is to be discarded, and not to be carried on one's back.

These *few* paragraphs at best are merely "a finger pointing to the moon." Please do not take the finger to be the moon and fix your intense gaze on the finger and thus miss all the splendor of heaven. After all, the usefulness of the finger is in "pointing away from itself to the light which illumines finger and all."

Artist of Life

TOWARD PERSONAL LIBERATION (JEET KUNE DO:V)

One cannot see a fight "as is," say from the point of view of a boxer, a wrestler, or anyone who is trained in a particular method, because he will see the fight according to the limits of his particular conditioning. Remember, every sport or art—this

includes judo, karate, and kung fu—every attempt to describe the fight is really "one's" version of it, a personal mental replica or a partial idea of the total fight, depending on his likes or dislikes.

Fighting is definitely not something dictated by your conditioning as a Korean martial artist, a Japanese martial artist, a Chinese martial artist, and so forth. While the wrestler ... could have either kicked or punched as a means to bridge the gap for his specialty, true observation begins when one is devoid of set pattern, and freedom of expression occurs when one is beyond system.

Similarly, a person cannot express himself fully—the important word here is *fully*—when a partial set structure or style is imposed on him. Combat "as is" is total (including all "that is" as well as "that is not"), without limiting boundaries or favorite lines, always alive, never set and constantly changing. It is not to be limited by your inclination, your physical makeup, or your environmental conditioning, although these are also parts of the total combat.

Source: Bruce Lee's essay entitled "Toward Personal Liberation (JKD)," circa 1971. Bruce Lee Papers.

If a person confines combat to a particular pattern, he can never express himself freely. For how can he express himself freely when there is a screen of his set pattern of what "should be" as opposed to the ever-changing "what is"? Because he does not want to be left uncertain or insecure, he "organizes" a choice pattern of combat, a drill-like precision of movements, a planned spontaneity, and so forth. From imitative drilling on such organized "land swimming patterns" the practitioner's margin of freedom of expression grows narrower and narrower. After all, the wrong means will lead to the wrong end. Consequently, it won't be long before the will becomes paralyzed within the framework of such a sterile pattern, ultimately accepting the limited pattern as total reality.

Many of our martial artists nowadays are merely performing their methodical routines as a response, rather than responding to "what is." They no longer "listen" to circumstances, they "recite" their circumstances. Within the Absolute there is just no distinction.

JKD: A New Style?

To set the record straight, I have NOT invented a "new" style, "composite," "modified," or otherwise; that is, set within a distinct form as apart from "this" method or "that" method. On the contrary, I hope to free my followers from clinging to styles, patterns, or molds. Remember that jeet kune do is merely a name used, a mirror in which we see ourselves. The brand name is nothing special.

What Is a Classical Style?

Unlike the traditional approach, there is never a series of rules, a classification of techniques, and so forth, that constitute a so-called JKD system/method of fighting. To begin with, there is no such thing as a system/method of fighting; although there is some sort of a progressive approach to training. To create a method of fighting is pretty much like [trying to] put a pound of water into wrapping paper and shape it. Its shape seems to depend on relationship.

In a way, water is a good example of JKD. Structurally, people tend to mistake JKD for a composite style because its efficiency lies in using any means to score, much like water finding its way to a crack. Because JKD is neither opposed to style nor not opposed

SECRET

JKD

(anytime when some other
writers write about Jeet Kune Do,
they write it according to their knowledge. this)

☒ Because one does not want to
be made uncertain or insecure,
so he organizes a pattern of
combat, a pattern of relationships
with his opponent, a pattern of pleasing
spontaneity, etc. etc. The more he
drilling on such organized pattern,
the practitioner margin of freedom of
paralyzed to the pattern and accept the pattern
as the real thing

One cannot really see a fight "as is" say from the point of view of a boxer, a "kicker" to

wrestler, or anyone who is taught by a particular method; because he will see the

fight according to the limits of his "particular conditioning". Fighting is not some-

thing dictated by your conditioning as a Chinese martial artist, a Japanese martial

artist, ect., ect. Take for instance the boxer: he will probably critisize the fact

that the two fighters are too close to allow crispy punching room. On the other hand,

the wrestler will complain that one of the fighter should crowd and smother the other's

"crispyness" thus be close enough to apply grappling tactics. So a split second

between the above two statements, the boxer could have switched into grappling tactics

when there is no punching room. The wrestler, when out of distance, could have kicked

or punched as a mean to bridge the gap for his specialty. True observation begins

when devoids of set patterns, and freedom of expression occurrs when one is beyond

systems.

One cannot "express" fully----the important word here is fully----when one is imposed

by a partial structure or style. For how can one be truly aware when there is a screen

of one's set pattern as opposed to "what is". What is is total (including what is and

what is not), without boundary, alive, always fresh and new.

to set the record straight, I have not invented a new style, that is, set within

distinct form as apart from 'this' style or 'that' style. On the contrary, I hope to free

my followers from styles. As I've mentioned, styles "set" and "trap" reality into a

choice mould. Freedom just cannot be preconceived, and where there is freedom, there

is neither good or its reaction bad. My only concerns are for those who are solidified

SECRET

to style, one can say it is outside as well as inside of all particular
structures and distinct styles. Also because JKD claims not to be
a style, some people concluded that maybe JKD is being neutral
or maybe simply indifferent. Again, this is not the case, for JKD is
both at once "this" and "not this." To fully understand, one must
transcend the duality of "for" and "against" into one organic whole.
A good martial artist rests in direct intuition.

Jeet Kune Do

173

What is a classical style of martial art? First and foremost, we must realize the fact that man created styles. Disregard the many romantic historical originations of the founder—by a wise old monk, by a special messenger in a dream or in a revelation, and so forth, and so on. A style should never be like a bible, the laws and principles of which can never be violated. So no matter what propaganda has been spread throughout the centuries, a classical style comes about as a result of a human being. Of course, being human beings, there will always be differences with regard to quality of training, physical makeup, level of understanding, environmental conditions, likes and dislikes, and so forth. Consequently, most classical styles were set up and accumulated from someone's chosen inclination under given circumstances.

The founder might be exposed to a partial truth, but as time goes by this partial truth becomes a sect, a law, or—worse still—a prejudicial faith. Furthermore, in order to pass along this "knowledge" from generation to generation, the various responses had to be organized and classified and presented in logical order. So what might have started off as some sort of personal fluidity on the part of its founder is now solidified knowledge, preserved and packaged for many younger generations as well as worldwide mass distribution, as well as mass indoctrination.

Because of the nature of organization and preservation, pretty soon the means become so elaborated that tremendous attention must be given to them, and pretty soon the end is forgotten. Of course, many more "different" styles would spring up, probably as a direct reaction to "the other's" truth. Each claims to possess the highest truth to the exclusion of all other styles. When one wants to study the tree, is it not futile to argue as to which single leaf, which design of branches, or which attractive flower one likes? For when you understand the root, you understand all its blossoming. By the way, plastic plants might look pretty—that is, if you like dead things.

The professed cure of a classical style is itself a disease. A style "sets" and "traps" partial reality into a choice mold. As a result, its practitioners are being enclosed within the style's limitation, which is definitely less than their own potential (discuss P.C.'s "control").

Many practitioners of the martial art are usually second-hand artists. They seldom learn to depend upon themselves for expression; rather, they faithfully follow an imposed pattern. To be sure, many of them have gained "routine efficiency" as prescribed/ outlined by that particular pattern. However, they have not come to understand themselves, for ultimately knowledge in martial art means self-knowledge. So one must not blindly follow a sterile pattern. Blindly following a sterile pattern would definitely cram and distort our natural growth. Instead, through self-exploration, flexible awareness, and self-expression one finds himself. Such self-knowledge is a continuing process, and the artist that possesses such quality expresses himself with the utmost freedom.

Freedom is something that cannot be preconceived, and fluidity is definitely not resisting the natural unrhythmic flow with one's partial set pattern. Remember that partial preformulated partiality lacks flexibility to cope with the ever-changing totality. Many different "stylists" have become desensitized, patternized robots. They become those organized forms, victims of conditioning handed down for thousands of years. A martial artist is never a replica of "this" style or "that" style. He is definitely not a product but a live individual, and remember, the individual is always more important than the system.

In traditional martial art, being wise seems to be a process of accumulation—like a white belt knows two sets, a brown belt has four sets, and so on. This is not true. In JKD the process is NOT that of accumulating fixed knowledge; rather it is a process of discovering the cause of ignorance. Most often it involves a shedding process, a sort of daily decrease rather than a daily increase. We must remember that freedom has always been with us, and it is not something to be gained toward the end through following some particular formula. We do not "become," we simply "are." The training in martial art is toward this end, of "being" mind, rather than "having" mind. Sterile pattern is incapable of such liveliness and freshness. Preformulations only limit and control the practitioner. Also, the mystical mind training promotes not the promised/so-called internal power, but psychological constipation. Whether it is inward or outward training, the JKD techniques are used to liberate the spirit rather than to bind the body.

Oftentimes the question is asked as to whether JKD is against form. In any physical movement there is always a most efficient and lively manner to carry it out, that is, regarding leverage, balance, economical use of motion, and so forth. However, live, efficient form is one thing, a sterile classical set that binds and conditions is another. Also, there is a subtle difference between "having no form" and having "no-form." The first is ignorance; the second, transcendence.

Truth is a pathless road. Jeet kune do is fresh red blood handed down in human veins and vessels. It is total awareness that has no "before" or "after." Thus it is not an organized institution that one can be a member of. Either you understand or you don't, and that is that. When I was teaching my Chinese system of gung fu, I had a system then. Upon my arrival in the States, I did have my "Chinese" Institute; but since then I no longer believe in systems (Chinese or not Chinese), nor organizations. Big organizations, domestic and foreign branches, affiliations, and so forth, are not necessarily the places where a martial artist discovers/finds himself. More often this is quite to the contrary. To reach the growing number of students, some sort of a pre-conformed set must be established as standards for the branches to follow. As a result, all members will be conditioned according to the prescribed system. Many will probably end up as prisoners of a systematized drill.

I believe in teaching/having a few pupils at one time, as teaching requires a constant alert observation of each individual in order to establish a direct relationship. A good teacher can never be fixed in a routine, and nowadays many are just that. During teaching, each moment requires a sensitive mind that is constantly changing and constantly adapting. Above all, a teacher must never force his student to fit his favorite pattern, [which] is a preformation. As a pointer of the way of truth, exposing his student's vulnerability, causing him to explore both internally (within) and externally, and finally integrating himself with his being. The process is much like caring for a ripening fruit, letting it happen. Fruit is fresh, juicy, and full of life. Of course, a plastic one might appear to be "more beautiful."

Many [martial] art instructors have said that martial art is life itself; however, I wonder how many of them really appreciate and truly understand. Without a doubt, life does not mean a partialized something, a frame. Life is a constant movement, unrhythmic movement, as well as constant change. Instead of flowing with this

change, many of the martial art leaders/"masters," past and present, have built an illusion of fixed forms, solidifying the ever flowing, dissecting the totality, organizing favorite patterns, planning spontaneity, separating the unity into duality of the soft versus the hard, and so forth. It is no wonder that our natural growth is blocked by the vain repetition of someone else's imposed pattern. Martial art is not simply the physical act of filling time and space through some sort of drill-/precision-like movement. Machines can do that, too. Nor is martial art a bunch of intellectual discourses or circus acts. A martial artist must be totally aware and capable of expressing himself creatively. His physical movement is his soul made visible. Indeed, martial art is the direct expression of the human soul.

Mechanical efficiency or manipulating skill is never as important as the exposure to our inward awareness. Remember, a martial artist is not merely the physical exponent of some prowess he may have been gifted with in the first place. As he matures, he will realize that his kick or punch is really not as much a tool to conquer his opponent, but a tool to explode through his consciousness, his ego, and all his mental blocks. Indeed, all the tools are ultimately means for penetrating the depth of his being so that he will achieve [and/or] regain this equilibrium of his inner center of gravity. With this inward vital loosening flows his outward expression of his tools. Behind each physical movement is his wholeness of being, this all-inclusive awareness.

Finally, a JKD man who says JKD is exclusively JKD is simply not in with it. He is still hung up on his self-closing resistance; in this case, he is anchored down in a reactionary pattern, and naturally he is still bound by another modified pattern and can move only within its limits. He has not digested the simple fact that truth exists outside of all molds and patterns, and awareness is never exclusive.

Again, let me remind you that JKD is merely just a name used, a boat to get one across, and once across, it is to be discarded, and not to be carried on one's back. These few paragraphs at best are merely a finger pointing to the moon. Please do not fix your gaze on the finger and miss all the heavenly glory. After all, the usefulness of the finger is in pointing away from itself to the light that illumines finger and all.

PARTIAL CONDITIONING (JEET KUNE DO:VI)

A person cannot see a fight "as is," say from the point of view of a boxer, a wrestler, or anyone who is trained in a particular method, because he will see the fight according to the limits of his particular conditioning. Every attempt to describe the fight is really one's "version" of it, a mental replica or a partial idea of the actual fight, depending on his likes and dislikes.

Fighting is definitely not something dictated by your conditioning as a Chinese martial artist, a Japanese martial artist, and so forth, nor is it something based on your likes and dislikes. Take for instance the case of the boxer: he probably will criticize the point that the two fighters are too close to allow "crispy" punching room. While the wrestler on the other hand will complain that one of the fighters should "crowd" and smother the other's "crispiness," thus being close enough to apply grappling tactics. So in a split second between the above two statements—when viewed from totality—the boxer could have switched into smothering grappling tactics when there is no crispy punching room. The wrestler, when out of distance, could have either kicked or punched as a means to bridge the gap for his specialty. True observation begins when one is devoid of set patterns, and freedom of expression occurs when one is beyond systems.

A person cannot see a fight "as is," say from the point of view of a boxer, a wrestler, or anyone who is trained in a particular method, because he will see the fight according to the limits of his particular conditioning.

A person cannot express himself fully—the important word here is *fully*—when a partial set structure or style is imposed on him. Fighting "as is" is total (including all "that is" as well as all "that is not"), without boundaries or lines, always alive and constantly changing. Now how can one have flexible awareness when

Source: Bruce Lee's essay entitled "Partial Conditioning," circa 1971. Bruce Lee Papers.

there is a screen of one's set pattern of "what should be" as opposed to "what is"? Set patterns just are not flexible enough for changes and adaptation. Because a person does not want to be

A person cannot express himself fully—the important word here is fully—when a partial set structure or style is imposed on him. Fighting "as is" is total (including all "that is" as well as all "that is not"), without boundaries or lines, always alive and constantly changing.

left uncertain or insecure, he "organizes" a choice pattern of combat, a pattern of artificial relationship with the opponent, a planned spontaneity, and so forth. From imitative drilling on such organized "land-swimming patterns" the practitioner's margin of freedom of expression grows narrower and narrower. The wrong means will lead to the wrong end, and it won't be long before he will become paralyzed within the framework of such patterns and will accept the limited patterns as reality, the unlimited. In fact, many martial artists are merely performing their methodical routines as response, rather than responding to "what is." They no longer "listen" to circumstances; they "recite THEIR circumstances."

Is JKD a New Style?

To set the record straight, I have NOT invented a new style or a modified style, that is, a style set within distinct form as apart from "this" method or "that" method. On the contrary, I hope to free my followers from styles, patterns, or molds. Jeet kune do is merely a name used, and through this analogy, a mirror in which to see ourselves.

In reality, the professed cure of a pattern is itself a disease, for it "sets" and "traps" reality into a choice mold. Just as one cannot get a piece of paper to wrap and shape water, fighting can never be made to conform to any one system. Freedom simply cannot be preconceived, and when there is freedom, there is neither good nor its reaction as bad. There are no distinctions within the Absolute.

My concerns are for those who are unknowingly being conditioned and solidified by a partialized and highly classical structure, gaining only "routine efficiency" rather than the freedom to express oneself. In most cases, they have become desensitized, patternized robots, listening to their own screams and loud yells.

They are those organized forms. They are those classical blocks. In short, they are the result of thousands of years of conditioning.

One should never look at combat from a certain angle, but from all possible angles. That is why in jeet kune do one is taught to utilize all ways and means to serve its end (efficiency is not the adherence to classical form; efficiency is anything that scores), but, and that is a rather important "but," he is bound by none. In other words, the structure of JKD, though possessed of all possible angles, is itself not possessed. The reason is simple: Any structure, however intelligently designed, becomes a cage if the student is obsessed with it. Thus a good student is one who is able to enter a mold but not be caged in it, to follow the principles, yet without being limited or bound by them. This is important, for a pliable, choiceless observation without exclusion is so essential in the cultivation of JKD. So what is important here is not to have an organized philosophy of combat, or, for that matter, a method of combat, but to observe neutrally what is taking place in actual combat, inwardly as well as outwardly.

JKD believes that freedom has always been with us, and [is] not something to be gained toward the end through some process of accumulation. We do not "become," we simply "are." The training is toward this, of "being" mind, rather than "having" mind. The trans-

formed state is merely a state of "being" and not a state of "becoming"; it is not an ideal, an end to be desired and achieved. Sterile pattern merely distorts and crams its practitioners and the mystical mind training promotes not internal power but psychological constipation. Whether it is inward or outward training, the JKD technique used is meant to liberate the spirit rather than to bind the body. To define JKD as a particular system (gung fu, karate, kickboxing, and so forth) is to miss the point completely. It is outside of all particular structures and distinct styles.

Definition: A Style Is a Classified Response to One's Chosen Inclination

Jeet kune do is never a method of classified techniques, but a means of total self-expression. There is never a series of rules, techniques, laws, principles, and so forth, that constitutes a system of fighting. For JKD is a process but not a goal, a constant movement rather than an established, fixed pattern; both the means and the end, to be sure, but never a means to an end. Many people mistake JKD for a composite style or being neutral or simply indifferent. This is not true, for it is both at once "this" and "not this." So JKD is neither opposed to styles nor not opposed to them. To understand, one must transcend the duality of "for" and "against"

Artist of Life

into one organic whole. A good JKD man rests in direct intuition.

People often mistakenly [believe] that JKD is against form. I don't think I'll go into detail on that, as other paragraphs will clarify that. One thing we must understand: that is, there is always a most efficient and alive manner to carry out a movement (and that the basic laws of leverage, body position, balance, footwork, and so forth, are not to be violated). However, alive, efficient form is one thing; sterile classical sets that bind and condition are another. Aside from the above mentioned, one must also distinguish the subtlety between "having no form" and having "no-form." The first is ignorance, the second transcendence.

The final aim of JKD is toward personal liberation. The instructions simply point the way to individual freedom and matured inwardness. Jeet kune do never imposes a set pattern on its practitioners. Mechanical efficiency or manipulatory skill is never as important as the inward awareness gained. Remember the fact that a martial art man is not merely a physical exponent of some prowess he may have been gifted with in the first place.[26]

As he matures, he will realize that his kick is really not so much a tool to conquer his opponent, but a tool to explode through his ego, his anger, his consciousness, and so forth. In fact, all the tools are ultimately means for penetrating the depth of his being, so that he will achieve this imperturbability of his inner center of gravity. With this inward vital loosening flows his outward expression of his tools. So we hear of such expressions as "it kicks" instead of "I kick." It simply means the kick is delivered with this wholeness of being, this all-inclusive attitude, without the utmost consciousness of the kicker. All the training is to round him up to be a complete man and not some sort of superman. To be a man of freedom is more important than to be a great fighter.

Truth is a pathless road. It is total expression that has no "before" or "after." Similarly, JKD is not an organized institution that one can be a member of. Either you understand or you don't, and that is that. I never believe in large organizations with their domestic and foreign branches, affiliations, honorary members, and so forth. To reach the masses, some sort of a preconformed, set system is required. As a result, the members are conditioned according to that system.

I believe in teaching just a few students, as teaching requires a constant alert observation on each individual in order to establish a direct relationship. A good teacher cannot be fixed in a routine, and many are just that. During teaching, each moment requires a sensitive mind that is constantly changing and constantly adapting. The teacher must never impose a lifeless pattern, a preformation, on his student. Thus unlike the traditional martial arts that are handed on by precepts of fixed forms, JKD can only be taught by personal and individual experiencing in the living present.

Instead of acceptance of change, many so-called leaders have built an illusion of fixed forms and the duality of the soft versus the hard. Our growth is blocked in this endless repetition of systematized pattern. Many martial art instructors have said that martial art is life itself; however, only a few really understand. To be sure, life does not mean stagnation, a sterile pattern, something lifeless. Life is a constant movement, unrhythmic movement. It is change, transformation, and all that. It is not enough to merely fill time and space through some sort of organized movements; machines can do that too.

A martial artist must express himself with the utmost freedom. He must be aware. His physical movement is his soul made visible. Indeed, martial art is the expression of the human soul.

In most cases, a practitioner of the martial art is a secondhand artist, a conformer. He seldom learns to depend upon himself for expression. Rather, he faithfully follows an imposed pattern. So as time goes by, he will probably understand some dead routines and be skillful according to that pattern, but he has not come to understand himself. In other words, he has gained control of the manipulative skill he has, but not control of what he is himself. Only self-knowledge in turn leads to freedom. A live person is not a molded reproduction of this style or that style. He is an individual, and the individual is always more important than the system.

Jeet kune do is not for anyone. I have taught many pupils, but very few become my disciples. Many of the students do not show their capability of understanding, nor the application of it in the right way, physically or mentally. Martial art must not be handed out indiscriminately to anyone; the student must be deserving of it. I seldom trust the black belters who knocked on the door for instruction. Wisdom to me is something sacred and I have great respect for it. Unless the prospect proves his worth and trust, I will not teach. It does not matter what his status is.

In martial art, many instructors derive their techniques and principles from intellectual theories and not from firsthand experience. Instructors like these can talk "about" combat, and there are many master talkers, but they cannot really teach it. They might create this law and that way, but the students under them will merely be conditioned and controlled rather than freeing themselves to be better artists. In truth, they are being enclosed within the system's limitation, which is definitely less than their own potential as live human beings. The more restricted a method, the lesser the opportunity for one's individual freedom of expression.

An excellent instructor is an excellent athlete. I am sure as he advances in age, he will be at a disadvantage with a good young man. However, he has no excuse not to be a superb artist among his contemporaries, physically and mentally. An unfit and inactive instructor might be of help to the mediocre students, but he can never truly feel or understand.

Finally, a JKD man who says JKD is exclusively JKD is simply not in with it. He is still hung up on his self-closing resistance; in this case he is anchored down to a reactionary pattern, and naturally he is still bound by another modified pattern and can only move within its limits. He has not digested the simple fact that truth exists outside of all molds and patterns, and awareness is never exclusive. Jeet kune do is merely a name used, a boat to get one across, and, once across, is to be discarded, and not carried on one's back. Let me also say that these few paragraphs at best are merely a finger pointing to the moon. Please do not take the finger to be the moon.

JKD (JEET KUNE DO:VII)

Anytime some other writers write about jeet kune do, they write about it according to their knowledge. One cannot see a fight "as is," say from the point of view of a boxer, a wrestler, or anyone who is trained in a particular method, because a person will see the fight according to the limits of his particular conditioning.

Fighting is not something dictated by your conditioning as a Chinese martial artist, a Japanese martial artist, and so forth, and so on. Take for instance the boxer: he will probably criticize the fact that the two fighters are too close to allow "crispy" punching room. On the other hand, the wrestler will complain that one of the fighters should crowd and smother the other's "crispiness," and thus be close enough to apply grappling tactics. So in a split second between the above two statements, the boxer could have switched into grappling tactics when there is no crispy punching room. The wrestler, when out of distance, could have kicked or punched as a means of bridging the gap for his specialty. True observation begins when one is devoid of set patterns, and freedom of expression occurs when one is beyond systems.

One cannot "express" fully—the important word here is *fully*—when one is imposed by a partial structure or style. For how can one be truly aware when there is a screen of one's set pattern as opposed to "what is?" What is total (including what is and what is not), without boundaries, and so forth. From drilling on such an organized "land swimming" pattern, the practitioner's margin of

Source: Bruce Lee's essay entitled "JKD," circa 1971. Bruce Lee Papers.

freedom of expression grows narrower and narrower. He becomes paralyzed within the framework of the pattern and accepts the pattern as the real thing. He no longer "listens" to circumstances, he "recites" his circumstances.

He is merely performing his methodical routine as [a] response rather than responding to what is. They are desensitized patternized robots, listening to their own screams and yells. They are those classical blocks; they are those organized forms; in short, they are the result of thousands of years of conditioning.

To set the record straight, I have not invented a new style, that is, set within a distinct form as apart from "this" style or "that" style. On the contrary, I hope to free my followers from styles. As I've mentioned, styles "set" and "trap" reality into a choice mold. Freedom just cannot be preconceived, and where there is freedom, there is neither good nor its reaction bad. My only concerns are for those who are conditioned and solidified by a partialized structure, who gain only routine efficiency, rather than freedom of individual expression.

Jeet kune do does not look at combat from a certain angle but from all possible angles. It utilizes all ways and means to serve its end, but, and that is a very important "but," it is bound by none; in other words, JKD, though possessed of all angles, is itself not possessed. This is because of the fact that any structure, however intelligently designed, becomes a cage if the practitioner is obsessed with it. This is where the value lies: the freedom both to use techniques and to dispense with them. Therefore, to define JKD as a particular system (gung fu, karate, and so forth) is to miss it completely. It is outside of all particular structures and distinct forms. However, do not mistake JKD for a composite style or being neutral or indifferent; for it is both at once "this" and "not this." It is neither opposed to styles nor not opposed to them. To understand one must transcend the duality of "for" and "against" into one organic whole. A good JKD man rests in direct intuition.

Truth is a pathless road. It is total expression that has no before or after. Similarly, JKD is not an organized institution that one can be a member of. Either you understand or you don't, and that is that. (There was a Jun Fan Gung Fu Institute, there was a method of wing chun, but there is no such organization or method existing now.)

Secondhand Artist

In most cases, a practitioner of the martial art is what I term as a secondhand artist, a conformer. To be sure, he seldom learns to depend upon himself for expression; rather, he faithfully follows a pattern. As time passes, he will probably understand some dead routines and be good according to his particularly set pattern, but he has not come to understand himself. Drilling on routines and set patterns will eventually make a person good according to the routines and set patterns, but only self-awareness and self-expression can lead to the truth. A live person is not a dead product of "this" style or "that" style; he is an individual, and the individual is always more important than the system.

In martial art, many instructors derive their techniques and principles from intellectual theories and not from application. He can talk about combat, and there are some master talkers, but he cannot really teach it. He might create this first law and that kicking principle, but the student will merely be conditioned and controlled rather than freeing himself to blossom into a better martial artist. Indeed, it is the "mold" and "system" that limits and interferes with reality.

As in any sport, we were told that five hundred years ago a martial artist could leap to a roof—by what means, check into the scientific application of high jumping in the Olympics—but of this I am certain: superior performances in martial art will rest in future development and not on many of the obsolete and outmoded training methods that exist.

An excellent instructor is an excellent athlete. True, I am sure as a person advances in age he will be at a disadvantage with a good young man, but he has no excuse not to be a first-rate man among his contemporaries, physically as well as mentally. An unfit and inactive instructor might be of some help to the mediocre student, but he can never truly understand.

Just as one cannot get a piece of paper to wrap and shape up water, fighting can never be made to conform to any one system, especially forcing it into a highly classical frame. Such a frame only kills and limits the life of the individual as well as the situation. The professed cure for such a frame is itself a disease. In the practice of JKD, there is no set or form, for JKD is not a method of classified techniques, laws, and so forth, that constitute a system of fighting. It does employ a systematic approach to training, but never a method of fighting. To go further, JKD is a process, not a goal; a means but not an end; a constant movement rather than an established, static pattern.

The final aim of JKD is toward personal liberation. It points the way to individual freedom and maturity. Mechanical efficiency or manipulatory skill is never as important as inward awareness gained, for to learn a movement without inward awareness results in imitative repetitiousness, a mere product. A true fighter "listens" to circumstances, while a classical man "recites" his circumstances. Remember that a martial art man is  not merely a physical exponent of some prowess he may have been gifted with in the first place. As he matures, he will realize that his side kick is really not so much a tool to conquer his opponent, but a tool to explode through his ego and all its follies. All that training is to round him up to be a complete man.

In essence, then, JKD seeks to restore the pupil to his primordial state so that he can "freely" express his own potential. The training consists of a minimum of form in the natural development of his tools toward the formless. In short, the idea is to be able to enter a mold yet not be caged in it, or to obey the principles without being bound by them. This is important, for a pliable, choiceless observation without exclusion is the foundation of a JKD man. An "altogether alert awareness" without a center or its circumference; to be in it, but not of it.

In closing, a JKD member who says JKD is exclusively JKD is simply not in with it. He is still hung up in his self-closing resis-

Artist of Life

tance; in this case, anchored down to a reactionary pattern. He is naturally still bound by another modified pattern and can move only within its limits. He has not digested the simple fact that truth exists outside of all molds and patterns, and awareness is never exclusive. Jeet kune do is merely a name used, a boat to get one across the river, and, once across, it is to be discarded, and not to be carried on one's back. Finally, let me also remind the readers that these few paragraphs are merely a finger pointing to the moon. Please do not take the finger to be the moon.

TOWARD PERSONAL LIBERATION (JKD:VIII)

The usefulness of a cup is in its emptiness, and the same can be said of a martial artist who has no form and is therefore devoid of "style" because he has no preconceived prejudices with regard to combat—no likes or dis-

likes. As a result, he is fluid, adaptable, and capable of transcending duality into one ultimate totality.

I hope you will be like the tea cup and join me in this brief talk together, and do venture with me lightly; that is, leave all the burdens of preconceived opinions and conclusions behind. On the other hand, do relate to what is being said to you because it is concerned with the blossoming of a martial artist, qua martial artist, and not "a Chinese martial artist," a "Japanese martial artist," a "Korean martial artist" or an "American martial artist," and so forth. A martial artist is first and foremost a human being, after all, which includes all of us. Nationalities, per se, have nothing to do with proficiency in martial art.

Let us imagine that several persons who are trained in different combative arts have just witnessed a fight. It is certain that each of them would relate a different account of it afterward. This is quite understandable, owing to the fact that one cannot see a fight "as is" since it will be viewed through the respective filters of a boxer, a wrestler, a karate-ka, a judo-ka, or anyone who is trained in a

Source: Bruce Lee's typed essay entitled "Jeet Kune Do—Toward Personal Liberation," plus Bruce Lee's handwritten note entitled "A Zen Story of Tea Serving," both circa 1971. Bruce Lee Papers.

particular method because they will see the fight according to the limits of their particular conditioning. Every attempt to describe the fight is really an intellectual reaction, a partialized idea of the total fight; in this case, depending on  one's likes and dislikes. However, in reality, the fight itself was not something dictated by your conditioning as a Korean martial artist, a Chinese martial artist, or whatever your style might happen to be. True observation begins when one is devoid of set patterns, and freedom of expression occurs when one is beyond systems.

A person cannot express himself fully and totally when a partial set structure or style is imposed upon him. Combat "as is" is total (including all "that is" as well as "that is not"), without favorite lines or angles, having no boundaries and always fresh and alive; it is never set and is constantly changing. Combat definitely must not be limited to your personal inclination, your physical makeup, or your environmental conditioning—although these are also parts of the totality of combat. Should there be any confinement of any sort, that is, putting combat into a chosen mold, there will always be a resistance of one's set pattern of "what should be" as opposed to the ever-changing "what is."

To set the record straight, I have not invented a new style, a composite, modified or otherwise, that is, set within a distinct form and laws as apart from "this" style or "that" method. On the contrary, I hope to free my followers from clinging to styles, patterns, or molds. So do remember that the term *jeet kune do* is merely a name used, a mirror in which we see ourselves. The name brand is nothing special.

Just what is a classical style of martial art? First and foremost, we must realize the fact that man created styles. Disregard the many fancy historical origins of their founders (for example, by a "wise ancient monk," by "special messenger in a dream," in a "holy revelation," and so forth): a style should never be the gospel truth, the laws and principles of which can never be violated. Man, the human being, is always more important than any style.

The founder of a style might have been exposed to some partial truth, but as time passed by, especially after the passing away of the founder, this partial truth became a law or, worse still, a prejudiced faith against the "different" sects. In order to pass along this knowledge from generation to generation, the various responses had to be organized and classified and presented in a logical order. So what might have started off as some sort of personal fluidity on the part of its founder is now solidified knowledge, a preserved cure-all for mass conditioning.

In the process the followers have made this knowledge not only a holy shrine, but a tomb in which the founder's wisdom is buried. Because of the nature of organization and preservation, the means would become so elaborated that tremendous attention must be given to them, and gradually the end is forgotten. The followers will then accept this "organized something" as the total reality of combat. Of course, many more "different" approaches would spring up, probably as a direct reaction to "the other's truth." Pretty soon these approaches too would become large organizations with each claiming to possess "truth" to the exclusion of all other styles. More and more the style becomes more important than its practitioner.

The professed cure of a classical style is itself a disease. A style has the tendency to "set" and "trap" reality into a preselected mold. Maybe because one does not want to be left uncertain or insecure he "organizes" a chosen pattern of combat. Disregard the cause; its followers are being enclosed and controlled within the style's limitation, which certainly limits their own potential. Like anything else, prolonged imitative drilling will promote mechanical precision; however, the margin of freedom of expression grows narrower and narrower. So one can follow formulas by "keeping his elbows in," "sinking his spirit down," "being this," or "being that," but in the long run, he will just be molded according to someone else's fancy. Remember, the whole is evidenced in all the parts, but an isolated part, efficient or not, does not constitute the whole. So one can say

Artist of Life

"a little learning is a dangerous thing" applies appropriately to those who are conditioned to a particular approach to combat.

If mere mechanical routine efficiency could make everyone a martial artist, then all would be well. Unfortunately, combat, like freedom, is something that cannot be preconceived. Preformations simply lack the flexibility to adapt to the ever changing. At this point, many would ask how then do we gain this unlimited freedom? I cannot tell you, because it will then become an approach. Although I can tell you what it is not, I cannot tell you what it is. "That," my friend, you will have to find out all by yourself, for there is no help but self-help. What is more, who says we have to "gain" freedom?

In traditional martial art, being wise seems to be a constant process of accumulating fixed knowledge—like a first degree black belt knows so many sets or techniques, a second degree a little more; or an X brand martial artist, a kicker, should accumulate Y brand's hand techniques, or vice versa. Accumulating fixed knowledge is not the process of JKD; rather, it is that of discovering the cause of ignorance, and oftentimes it involves a shedding process. Remember my friends that ultimately, knowledge in martial art simply means self-knowledge, and JKD can become intelligible only in the process of self-discovery.

Freedom has always been with us, and it is not something to be gained at the end through following some particular formulas. We do not "become," we simply "are." So the training in JKD is toward this: "being" mind, rather than "having" mind. Sterile patterns are incapable of such liveliness and freshness, and preformations only squelch creativity and impose mediocrity. Also, the mystical mind training promotes not the promised internal power but psychological constipation. In JKD, whether it is inward or outward training, the techniques used are often temporary expedients, the aim being to liberate the spirit rather than to bind the body.

Unlike the traditional approach, there is never a series of rules, a classification of techniques, and so forth, which constitute a so-called JKD method of fighting. To begin with, there is no such thing as a method of fighting. To create such a method is pretty much like trying to contain and shape a pound of water in wrapping paper (and then attempting to argue which is the "best" color or texture of the wrapping paper).

Briefly, JKD is not a form of special conditioning with a set of beliefs and a particular approach. So basically it is not a "mass" art. It does not look at combat from a certain angle but from all possible angles because it is not based on any system. Although it utilizes all ways and means to serve its end (efficiency is anything that scores), it is bound by none, and it is therefore free from these ways and means. In other words, JKD, though possessed of all angles, is itself not possessed; for any structure, however efficiently designed, becomes a cage if the practitioner is obsessed with it.

To define JKD as a style (that is, gung fu, karate, kickboxing, and so forth) is to miss the point completely. If JKD is not a style or a method, maybe it is being neutral or maybe it is indifference. However, this is not the case either, for JKD is both at once "this" and  "not this," and JKD is neither opposed to styles nor not opposed to them. To understand fully, one must transcend the duality of "for" and "against" into one organic whole. Within the Absolute there is simply no distinction; everything is. A good JKD artist rests in direct intuition.

When I first arrived in the United States I was teaching my version of wing chun—I had my "Chinese" system then. However, since then I no longer am interested in systems or organization. Organized institutes tend to produce patternized prisoners of a systematized concept, and the instructors are often fixed in a routine. Of course, what is worse is that forcing the members to fit a lifeless preformation blocks their natural growth. A teacher, a good teacher that is, functions as a pointer to truth, but not a giver of truth. He employs a minimum of form to lead his student to the formless. Furthermore, he points out the importance of

Artist of Life

being able to enter a mold without being imprisoned by it; or to follow the principles without being bound by them.

A pliable, choiceless observation without exclusion is so essential in JKD, or martial art, an "altogether alert awareness" without

its center or its circumference; to be in it, but not of it. Above all, I believe a teacher does not depend on a method and drill systematic routines; instead, he studies each individual student and awakens him to explore himself, both internally and externally, and ultimately integrate himself with his being. Such teaching, which is really no teaching, requires a sensitive mind with great flexibility, and it is difficult to come by nowadays.

Sincere and serious learners are equally difficult to come by. Many of them are five-minute enthusiasts, some of them come in with ill intentions, but unfortunately, most of them are secondhand artists, basically conformers. The second-hand artist seldom learns to depend upon himself for expression; instead, he faithfully follows an imposed pattern. So what is nurtured is the dependent mind rather than independent inquiry. As time goes by he might understand some routines and might even be skillful according to a particular pattern. However, he has gained control of manipulative skill, but he has not gained an understanding of what he is in himself.

Martial art is not merely the physical act of filling time and space with precision-like movements. Machines can do that, too. As he matures, a martial artist will realize that his kick or punch is really not so much a tool to conquer his opponent, but a tool to explode through his consciousness, his ego, and all mental obstacles. Indeed, the tools are ultimately a means for penetrating the depth of his being so that he will restore the equilibrium of his inner center of gravity. With this vital inward loosening flows his outward expression of his tools. Behind each physical movement of an accomplished martial artist is this wholeness of being, this all-inclusive attitude.

How often we are told by different "masters" and "professors" (and it would seem that we do have a lot of philosophical and sometimes scholastic professors around) that martial art is "life itself." I wonder how many of them really appreciate that statement and truly understand. To be sure, life does not mean a partialized something, a frame. Life is never stagnation. It is a constant movement, unrhythmic movement, as well as constant change. Instead of flowing with this change without prejudice, many of the martial art "masters—past and present—have built an illusion of fixed forms, solidifying the ever flowing, dissecting the totality, organizing select patterns, planning spontaneity, separating the harmonious unity into duality of the soft versus the firm, grappling versus long range, and so forth.

The result of this is quite evident today; we now have many, many insensitive, patternized robots around listening to their own screams and spiritual yells. They are merely performing their methodical routines as potential responses rather than responding to "what is." They no longer listen to circumstances; they "recite their circumstances." These poor souls have become those orga-

Artist of Life

nized forms, they are those classical blocks; in short, they are the "product" of conditioning handed down hundreds and thousands of years ago.

Often the question is asked whether JKD is against forms. It is true that there are no prearranged sets or kata in JKD. However, in any physical movement there is always a most efficient and alive manner for each individual to accomplish the purpose of the performance, that is, in regard to proper leverage, balance in movement, economical and efficient use of motion and energy, and so forth. Live, efficient movement that liberates is one thing; sterile classical sets that bind and condition are another. Also there is a subtle difference between "having no form" and having "no-form"; the first is ignorance, the second transcendence.

There is no standard in total combat, and expression must be free. This liberating truth becomes reality only in proportion to its being experienced and lived in its suchness by the individual himself. And this truth is far beyond styles or disciplines.

Remember too that JKD is just a name used, a vehicle to carry you over obstacles, like a boat used to get one across a river. Once across, the boat is to be discarded, not carried on one's back. These few paragraphs are, at best, merely "a finger pointing to the moon." Please do not focus on the finger or you will not see the moon, and thus you will miss all the heavenly glory. After all, the usefulness of the finger is in "pointing away from itself to the light which illuminates finger and all."

5-J

NOTES ON JEET KUNE DO

In martial art cultivation there must be a sense of freedom. A conditioned mind is never a free mind.

Conditioning limits a person within the framework of a particular system.

There is the mere repetition of rhythmic, calculated movements that has the "aliveness" and "as-it-isness" taken away from it. It becomes an anchorage that holds and ties down, an accumulation of more and more forms, one form from here and one form from there (modification of conditioning), means and ends.

Relationship is understanding.

[The] more and more you [are] aware, the more and more you shed from day to day what you have learned so that your mind is always fresh, uncontaminated by previous conditioning.

Truth is your relationship with the opponent; it is constant movement with. It is "living"; it is never static.

Form is the cultivation of resistance, exclusive drilling on a pattern of choice. Instead of creating resistance, enter straight into the movement as it arises. Do not condemn or like—unprejudiced awareness can lead to reconciliation with the opponent in a total understanding of what is.

[The] more and more you [are] aware, the more and more you shed from day to day what you have learned so that your mind is always fresh, uncontaminated by previous conditioning.

Source: Bruce Lee's handwritten paper entitled "Notes on Jeet Kune Do," circa 1971. Bruce Lee Papers.

Artist of Life

Isolation in an Enclosed Pattern

Once conditioned in a partialized method, the practitioner faces his opponent through a screen of resistance—actually, he is "performing" his stylized blocks and listening to his own screaming, and not to what the opponent is really doing.

To fit in with his opponent a person should have direct perception—there is no direct perception where there is resistance, a "this is THE only true way" attitude.

Having the TOTALITY means [being] capable of following along with what is, because what is constantly moving and constantly changing, and if one is anchored down to one partialized view, one will not be able to follow the swift movement of what is.

Whatever one's opinion about the advisability of making hooking and swinging part of one's style, there cannot be the least argument about the necessity of acquiring perfect defenses against it. Indeed, nearly all natural fighters do that (versatility to one's attack)—you must hit from wherever the hand is.

The system becomes important—and not the human being!

To know oneself is to study oneself in action with another person.

To understand combat, one must approach it in a very simple and direct manner.

Relationship is a process of self-revelation. Relationship is the mirror in which you discover yourself—to be is to be related.

Set-pattern is incapable of adaptability, of pliability—offering you a better cage.

TRUTH IS OUTSIDE OF ALL PATTERNS.

Forms: vain repetition which offers an orderly and beautiful escape from self-knowledge with an alive opponent.

Accumulation is self-enclosing resistance, and flowery techniques strengthen the resistance.

MORE NOTES ON JEET KUNE DO

Freedom is something that cannot be preconceived. To realize freedom requires an alert mind, a mind that is deep with energy, a mind that is capable of immediate perception without the process of graduation, without the idea of an end to be slowly achieved.

The margin of freedom for the classical practitioner is getting narrower all the time.

There is no condemnation, no demand for a pattern of action in understanding. You are merely observing—just look at it and watch it. The perceiving mind is living, moving, full of energy, and only such a mind can understand what truth is.

Classical methods and tradition make the mind a slave—you are no longer an individual, but merely a product. Your mind is the result of a thousand yesterdays.

Life is wide, limitless—there is no border, no frontier.

Not conviction, not method, but perception is the way of truth. It is a state of effortless awareness, pliable awareness, choice-less awareness.

The moment you have a center, there must also be a circumference; and to function from a center, within a circumference, is slavery.

Source: Bruce Lee's handwritten essay entitled "More Notes on Jeet Kune Do." Bruce Lee Papers.

Artist of Life

It is an "altogether" feeling, without a center.

Wipe away and dissolve all experience and be "born afresh."

When you listen further to something, you have ceased to listen. Knowing is a constant movement; therefore there is no static state, no fixed point from which to act. Knowledge is binding, but the movement of knowing is not binding.

Life is something for which there is no answer; it must be understood from moment to moment. The answer we find inevitably conforms to the pattern of what we think we know.

Simplicity is an inward state of being in which there is no contradiction, no comparison; it is the quality of perception in approaching any problem. It is not simply when the mind approaches any problem with a fixed idea or belief, or with a particular pattern of thought.

A simple mind, surely, is one that functions, that thinks and feels without a motive. Where there is a motive, there must be a way, a method, a system of discipline. The motive is brought about by the desire for an end, for a goal, and to achieve that goal, there must be a way, and so forth. Meditation is a freeing of the mind from all motives.

Because one does not want to be disturbed, to be made uncertain, he establishes a pattern of conduct, of thought, a pattern of relationship to man, and so forth. Then he becomes a slave to the pattern and takes the pattern to be the real thing.

Any effort the mind makes will further limit the mind, because effort implies the struggle toward a goal; and when you have a goal, a purpose, an end in view, you have placed a limit on the mind, and it is with such a mind that you are trying to meditate.

This evening I see something totally new, and that nervousness is experienced by the mind; but tomorrow that experience becomes mechanical, because I want to repeat the sensation, the pleasure of it. The description is never real. What is real is seeing the truth instantaneously, because truth has no future.

Observe what is with undivided awareness.

Meditation, surely, can never be a process of concentration, because the highest form of thinking is negative thinking. Negation is not the opposite of the positive, but a state in which there is neither the positive nor its reaction as the negative. It is a state of complete emptiness.

Concentration is a form of exclusion; and where there is exclusion, there is a thinker who excludes. It is the thinker, the excluder, the one who concentrates, who creates contradiction, because then there is a center from which there can be a deviation, a distraction.

Awareness has no frontier; it is a giving of your whole being toward something, without exclusion.

Concentration is a narrowing down of the mind—but we are concerned with the total process of living, and to concentrate exclusively on any particular aspect of life belittles life.

How can there be methods and systems by which to arrive at something that is living? To that which is static, fixed, dead, there can be a way, a definite path, but not to that which is living. Do not reduce reality to a static thing, and then invent methods by which to reach it.

Acceptance, denial, and conviction prevent understanding. Let your mind and the speaker's mind move together in understanding, with sensitivity; then there is a possibility of real communion with each other. To understand, surely, there must be a state of choiceless awareness in which there is no sense of comparison or condemnation, no waiting for a further development of the thing we are talking about in order to agree or disagree. Don't start from a conclusion above all.

Understanding requires not just a moment of perception, but a continuous awareness, a continuous state of inquiry in which there is no conclusion. There is no thinking that is free— all thought is partial; it can never be total. Thought is the response of memory, and memory is always partial, because memory is the result of experience; so thought is the reaction of a mind which is conditioned by experience.

KNOWLEDGE, surely, is always of time, whereas KNOWING is not of time. KNOWLEDGE is from a source, from an accumulation, from a conclusion, while KNOWING IS A MOVEMENT.

The additive process is merely a cultivation of memory, which becomes mechanical. Learning is never cumulative; it is a movement of knowing that has no beginning and no end.

There is an awareness without choice, without any demand, an awareness in which there is no anxiety; and in that state of mind there is perception. It is the perception alone that will resolve all our problems.

A state of perception and nothing else—that is, a state of being.

Action is our relationship to everything.

Action is not a matter of right and wrong. It is only when action is partial, not total, that there is right and wrong.

Not the cultivated innocence of a clever mind that wants to be innocent, but that state of innocence in which there is no denial or acceptance, and in which the mind just sees what IS.

We shall find the truth when we examine the problem. The problem is never apart from the answer; the problem is the answer—the understanding of the problem is the dissolution of the problem.

WHEN THE MIND IS TETHERED TO A CENTER, NATURALLY IT IS NOT FREE; IT CAN MOVE ONLY WITHIN THE LIMITS OF THAT CENTER.

If one is isolated, he is dead; he is paralyzed within the fortress of his own ideas.

The mind must be wide open in order to function freely in thought. For a limited mind cannot think freely.

A concentrated mind is not an attentive mind, but a mind that is in the state of awareness can concentrate. Awareness is never exclusive; it includes everything.

5-L

ADDITIONAL NOTES ON JEET KUNE DO

Jeet kune do is not a "method of concentration or meditation." It is "being." It is an "experience," a "way" that is "not a way."

Jeet kune do seeks "enlightenment," which results from the resolution of all subject-object relationships and oppositions in a pure void (that is not void)—" enlightenment" is not an experience or activity of a thinking and self-conscious subject.

Jeet kune do is the awareness of "pure being" (beyond subject and object), an immediate grasping of being in its "thusness" and "suchness" (not "particularized reality").

Mind is an ultimate reality that is aware of itself and is not the seat of our empirical consciousness—by "being" mind instead of "having" mind ("no mind and no-mind;" "no form and no-form").

Converge with all that is.

To think that this insight is a subjective experience that is "attainable" by some kind of process of mental purification is to doom oneself to error and absurdity—"mirror-wiping Zen."

It is not a technique of introversion by which one seeks to exclude matter and the external world, to eliminate distracting thoughts, to sit in silence emptying the mind of images, and to concentrate on the purity of one's own spiritual essence. Zen is not a mysticism of "introversion" and "withdrawal." It is not "acquired contemplation."

Source: Bruce Lee's handwritten essay entitled "Additional Notes on Jeet Kune Do." Bruce Lee Papers.

Do not separate mediation as a means *(dhyana)* from enlightenment as an end *(Prajna)*—the two are really inseparable, and the Zen discipline consisted of seeking to realize this wholeness and unity of prajna and dhyana in all one's actions.

The Three Faults
1. The invention of an empirical self that observes itself
2. Viewing one's thought as a kind of object or possession, situating it in a separate, isolated "part of itself"—I "have" a mind
3. The striveing to wiping the mirror

This clinging and possessive ego-consciousness, seeking to affirm itself in "liberation," craftily tries to outwit reality by rejecting the thoughts it "possesses" and emptying the mirror of the mind, which it also "possesses"—emptiness itself is regarded as a possession and an "attainment."

There is no enlightenment to be attained and no subject to attain it.

Zen is not "attained" by mirror-wiping meditation, but by "self-forgetfulness in the existential 'present' of life here and now." We do not "come," we "are." Don't strive "to become," but be.

The void (or the unconscious) may be said to have two aspects: (1) It simply is what it is. (2) It is realized, it is aware of itself, and to speak improperly, this awareness is "in us," or better, we are in it.

It is to see things as they are and not to become attached to anything—to be unconscious means to be innocent of the working of a relative (empirical) mind.

Being Unbound
WHEN THERE IS NO ABIDING OF THOUGHT ANYWHERE ON ANYTHING—THIS IS BEING UNBOUND. This NOT ABIDING ANYWHERE is the root of our life.

Prajna is not self-realization, but realization pure and simple, beyond subject and object.

To see where there is no something (object)—this is true seeing. The seeing is the result of having nothing to stand on. It is simply "pure seeing," beyond subject and object, and therefore "no-seeing."

Zen liberates the mind from servitude to imagined spiritual states as "objects" that too easily become hypostatized and turn into idols that obsess and delude the seeker.

Pure Seeing

"No-seeing" and "no-mind" are not renunciations, but fulfillment. The seeing that is without subject or object is "pure seeing."

The direct awareness in which is formed "truth that makes us free"—not the truth as an object of knowledge, but the truth lived and experienced in concrete and existential awareness.

The direct awareness in which is formed "truth that makes us free"—not the truth as an object of knowledge, but the truth lived and experienced in concrete and existential awareness.

What is Art?

Art is communication of feelings.

Art must originate with an experience or feeling of the artist.

Much pseudo-art comes from insincerity or the attempt to create a work of art that does not grow from actual experience or feeling.

Adequate form requires INDIVIDUALITY rather than imitative repetitiousness, brevity rather than bulkiness, clarity rather than obscurity, SIMPLICITY OF EXPRESSION RATHER THAN COMPLEXITY OF FORM.

THE ULTIMATE SOURCE OF JEET KUNE DO

The Enlightenment

It is being itself, in becoming itself. Reality in its-isness, the "isness" of a thing. Thus isness is the meaning—having freedom in its primary sense—not limited by attachments, confinements, partialization, complexities.

Morally

Teaches us not to look backward once the course is decided upon.

Philosophically

Treats life and death indifferently Jeet kune do is not to hurt, but it is one of the avenues through which life opens up its secrets to us).

Source: Bruce Lee's handwritten essay entitled "The Ultimate Source of Jeet Kune Do," circa 1971. Bruce Lee Papers.

The fighter is to be always single-minded with one object in view: to fight, looking neither backward nor sidewise. Rid obstructions to one's onward movement—emotionally, physically or intellectually.

A way of life, a system of willpower and control, though it ought to be enlightened by intuition.

To approach jeet kune do with the idea of mastering the will.

Forget about winning and losing, forget about pride and pain: let your opponent graze your skin and you smash into his flesh; let him smash into your flesh and you fracture his bones; let him fracture your bones and you take his life! Do not be concerned with your escaping safely—lay down your life before him!

The Tools (Your Natural Weapons) Have a Double Purpose

a.   To destroy the opponent in front of you—annihilation of things that stand in the way of peace, justice, and humanity.

b.   To destroy your own impulses from the instinct of self-preservation (anything that is bothering your mind)— not to hurt or maim anyone but one's own greed, anger, and folly. In this respect, jeet kune do is directed toward oneself.

The punch and kicks are tools to kill the ego. The tools represent the force of intuitive or instinctive directness, which, unlike the intellect or the complicated, does not divide itself, blocking its own freedom. The tools move onward without looking backward or sideways.

The tools stand as symbols of the invisible spirit keeping the mind, body, and limbs in full activity.

The Abiding Stage (Letting Go Itself from Itself)

The point where the mind stops to abide—the attachment to an object, the stop of the flow. Not allowing your attention to be arrested. To transcend the dualistic comprehension of the situation.

Prajna Immovable

Prajna immovable doesn't really mean immovability or insensitivity but that the mind itself is endowed with infinite mobilities that know no hindrances.

Artist of Life

Prajna immovable is the destroyer of delusion. Not to move means not to "stop" with an object that is seen. "The One Mind." "Nonassertiveness."

Jeet kune do dislikes "partialization" or "localization." Totality meets all situations.

Fluidity of mind—the moon in the stream—where it is at once movable and immovable.

Any space between two objects where something else can enter.

The "tools" are at an "undifferentiated center of a circle that has no circumference."

Moving and yet not moving, in tension and yet relaxed, seeing everything that is going on and yet not at all anxious about the way it may turn, with nothing purposely designed, nothing consciously calculated, no anticipation, no expectation—in short, standing innocently like a baby and yet with all the cunning and subterfuge of the keenest intelligence of a fully matured mind.

The delusive mind is the mind intellectually and effectively burdened. It thus cannot move on from one move to another without stopping and reflecting on itself, and this obstructs its native fluidity—creating.

Fluidity is nonhindrance to follow its course like water.

The wheel revolves when it is not too tightly attached to the axle. When the mind is tied up, it feels inhibited in every move it makes, and nothing will be accomplished with any sense of spontaneity. Not only that, the work itself will be of a poor quality, or it may not be finished at all.

Recollection and anticipation are fine qualities of consciousness that distinguish the human mind from that of the lower animals. They are useful and serve certain purposes, but when actions are directly related to the problem of life and death recollection and anticipation must be given up so that they will not interfere with the fluidity of mentation and the lightning rapidity of action.

Jeet kune do's aggressive mental training is not a mere philosophical contemplation of the effervescence of life or a frozen type of mold, but an entrance into the realm of nonrelativity, and it is real.

The point is to utilize the art as a means to advance in the study of the Way.

To be on the alert means to be deadly serious; to be deadly serious means to be sincere to oneself, and it is sincerity that finally leads to the Way.

Nirvana

To be consciously unconscious, or to be unconsciously conscious is the secret of Nirvana. The act is so direct and immediate that intellection finds no room here to insert itself and cut it to pieces.

A struggle of any nature can never be settled satisfactorily until the absolute fact is touched. Where neither opponent can affect the other, not neutrality, not indifference, but TRANSCENDENCE is the thing needed.

Ultimately jeet kune do is not a matter of technology, but of spiritual insight and training.

It is the ego that stands rigidly against things coming from the outside, and it is this "ego rigidity" that makes it impossible for us to accept everything that confronts us.

Art lives where ABSOLUTE FREEDOM is, because where it is not, there can be no creativity.

To be of no mind means the "everyday mind."

Because your self-consciousness or ego-consciousness is too conspicuously present over the entire range of your attention—which fact interferes with a free display of whatever proficiency you have so far acquired or are going to acquire. You should get rid of this obtruding self—or ego-consciousness—and apply yourself to the work to be done as if nothing particular were taking place at the moment.

The waters are in motion all the time, but the moon retains its serenity. The mind moves in response to the ten thousand situations but remains ever the same.

The Pristine Purity

In order to display its native activities to the utmost limit, remove all physic obstruction.

Sharpen the psychic power of seeing in order to act immediately in accordance with what the mind sees—the seeing takes place with the inner mind.

Learning gained is learning lost.

The knowledge and skill you have achieved are after all meant to be "forgotten" so you can float in emptiness without obstruction and comfortably. Learning is important, but do not become its slave. Above all, do not harbor anything external and superfluous; the mind is the primary.

You can never be the master of your technical knowledge unless all your psychic hindrances are removed and you can keep the mind in the state of emptiness (fluidity), even purged of whatever technique you have obtained—with no conscious effort.

With all the training thrown to the wind, with a mind perfectly unaware of its own workings, with the self vanishing nowhere anybody knows, the art of jeet kune do attains perfection.

Learning the techniques corresponds to an intellectual apprehension in Zen of its philosophy, and in both Zen and jeet kune do a proficiency in this does not cover the whole ground of the discipline. Both require us to come to the attainment of ultimate reality, which is the emptiness or the absolute. The latter transcends all modes of relativity. In jeet kune do, all the technique is to be forgotten, and the unconscious is to be left alone to handle the situation—when the technique will assure its wonders automatically or spontaneously—to float in totality. To have no technique is to have all technique.

Any technique, however worthy and desirable, becomes a disease when the mind is obsessed with it.

The Six Diseases
1. The desire for victory
2. The desire to resort to technical cunning
3. The desire to display all that you have learned
4. The desire to overawe the enemy
5. The desire to play a passive role
6. The desire to get rid of whatever disease you are likely to be infected with

"To desire" is an attachment. "To desire not to desire" is also an attachment. To be unattached, then, means to be free at once from both statements, positive and negative. In other words, this is to be simultaneously both "yes" and "no," which is intellectually absurd.

However, not so in Zen!

The undifferentiated center of a circle that has no circumference: The jeet kune do man should be on the alert to meet the interchangeability of the opposites. But as soon as his mind "stops" with either of them, it loses its own fluidity. A jeet kune do man should keep his mind always in a state of emptiness so that his freedom in action will never be obstructed.

When there is no obstruction of whatever kind the jeet kune do man's movements are like flashed lightning or like the mirror reflecting images.

The spirit is no doubt the controlling agent of our existence (as to its whereabouts we can never tell), although it is altogether beyond the realm of corporeality. This invisible seat controls every movement in whatever external situation it may happen to find itself. It is thus extremely mobile, no "stopping" in any place at any moment.

Preserve the state of spiritual freedom and nonattachment as soon as he assumes the jeet kune do stance.

"The Master of the House": To Make the Tools See

All movements come out of emptiness, and the mind is the name given to this dynamic aspect of emptiness, and further that here is no crookedness, no ego-centered motivation, as the emptiness is sincerity, genuineness, and straightforwardness allowing nothing between itself and its movements.

Jeet kune do consists in your not seeing me and my not seeing you—where Yin and Yang have not yet differentiated themselves.

While walking or resting, sitting or lying, while talking or remaining ... quiet, while eating or drinking, do not allow yourself to be indolent, but be most arduous in search of "THIS."

Instead of looking directly into the fact, cling to forms (theories) and go on entangling yourself further and further, finally putting yourself into an inextricable snare.

We do not see IT in its suchness because of our indoctrination, crooked and twisted.

Discipline in conformity with the nature.

The process of maturing does not mean to become a captive of conceptualization. It is to come to the realization of what lies in our innermost selves.

Artist of Life

The great mistake is to anticipate the outcome of the engagement; you ought not to be thinking of whether it ends in victory or in defeat. Just let Nature take its course, and your tools will strike at the right moment.

Jeet Kune Do

1. The absence of a system of stereotyped techniques
2. The "fitting in" spirit
3. Scratch away all the dirt our being has accumulated and reveal reality in its is-ness, or in its suchness, or in its nakedness, which corresponds to the Buddhist concept of emptiness

Because of the pure-heartedness and empty-mindedness (wu wei) of a man, his "tools" partake of this quality and play their role with the utmost degree of freedom.

Jeet kune do, ultimately, is not a matter of petty technique but of highly developed personal spirituality and physique.

It is not a question of developing what has already been developed but of recovering what has been left behind—although this has been with us, in us, all the time and has never been lost or distorted except for our misguided manipulation of it.

While being trained in jeet kune do, the student is to be active and dynamic in every way. But in actual combat, his mind must be calm and not at all disturbed. He must feel as if nothing critical is happening. When he advances, his steps are light and secure, and his eyes are not glaringly fixed on the enemy as those of an insane man might be. His behavior is not in any way different from his everyday behavior. No change is taking place in his expression. Nothing betrays the fact that he is now engaged in a mortal fight.

Technical skill is to be subordinate to the psychic training, which will finally raise the practitioner even to the level of high spirituality.

A jeet kune do man faces reality, and not crystallization of form. The tool is a tool of formless form.

No-abode means that the ultimate source of all things is beyond human understanding, beyond the categories of time and space. As it thus transcends all modes of relativity, it is called "having no abode," to which any possible predications are applicable.

He is no more himself. He moves as a kind of automaton. He has given himself up to an influence outside his everyday consciousness, which is no other than his own deeply buried unconscious, whose presence he was never hitherto aware of.

Art is never decoration, embellishment; instead it is the work of enlightenment. Art, in other words, is a technique for acquiring liberty.

Jeet kune do became known as the art "not founded on techniques or doctrines"—just as you are.

Absence of thought: the mind should be freed from the influence of the external world, to let the mind take its course unhindered among phenomena.

To bring the mind into sharp focus and to make it alert so that it can immediately intuit truth, which is everywhere, the mind must be emancipated from old habits, prejudices, restrictive thought process, and even ordinary thought itself.

Three Components

Absence of thought is the doctrine: And it means not to be carried away by thought in the process of thought—not to be defiled by external objects—to be in thought yet devoid of thought.

"Absence of Stereotyped Technique" as the substance in order to be total and free.

Nonattachment as the foundation.

All lines and movements are the function.

It is man's original nature—in its ordinary process, thought moves forward without a halt; past, present, and future thoughts continue as an unbroken stream.

Absence means freedom from duality and all defilements.

Thought means thought of thusness and self-nature.

True thusness is the substance of thought, and thought is the function of true thusness.

To meditate means to realize the imperturbability of one's original nature. Meditation means to be free from all phenomena, and calmness means to be internally unperturbed. There will be calmness when one is free from external objects and is not perturbed.

True thusness is without defiling thought; it cannot be known through conception and thought.

Artist of Life

There is no thought except that of the true thusness. Thusness does not move, but its motion and function are inexhaustible.

The mind is originally without activity; the Way is always without thought.

By knowledge is meant knowing the emptiness and tranquility of the mind.

Insight means realizing that your original nature is not created.

Being empty means having no appearance: having no style or form to let one's opponent work on.

Being tranquil means not having been created in its thusness; not being created means not having any illusions or delusions.

No cultivation does not really mean the absence of any kind of cultivation. What it signifies is a "cultivation by means of non-cultivation." To practice cultivation through cultivation is to act with conscious mind, that is to say, to practice assertive activity.

Separation

Separation is inexpressible because as soon as one tries to express it, what one expresses is itself a thing, which means that by so doing one remains in the state of being linked with things.

Just as yellow leaves may be taken as gold coins in order to stop the crying of children, thus the so-called secret moves and contorted postures do not mean doing nothing at all, but only to have no deliberate mind in whatever one does.

Have no mind that selects or rejects; to be without deliberate mind is to have no thoughts.

There is no need to exert oneself in special cultivation outside the daily round of living. There is no difference between such enlightenment and what is ordinarily termed knowledge, for in the latter a contrast exists between the knower and the known; whereas in the former there can be no such contrast.

The Two Diseases
1. One is riding an ass to search for an ass.
2. One is riding an ass and being unwilling to dismount.

There are styles that favor straight lines; then there are styles that favor round line circles. Styles that cling to one partial aspect of combat are in bondage. Jeet kune do is a technique for acquiring liberty—it is the work of enlightenment. Art is never decoration or embellishment. A choice method, however exacting, fixes its practitioners in a pattern (combat is never fixed, but changes from moment to moment). It is basically a practice of resistance. Such practice leads to clogginess, and understanding is not possible, and its adherents are never free because the Way of combat is not based on personal choice and fancies. The truth of the Way of combat is perceived from moment to moment, and only when there is awareness without condemnation, justification, or any form of identification.

Jeet kune do favors formlessness so that it can assume all forms, and since it has no style, therefore jeet kune do fits in with all styles. As a result, jeet kune do uses all ways and is bound by none, and likewise it uses any techniques or means that serve its end. In this art, efficiency is anything that scores.

Many martial artists like "more," like "different," not knowing what the truth and the Way exhibit in the simple everyday movements, because it is here they miss these things (if there is any secret, it is missed by seeking). The physical-bound goes for puffing

Artist of Life

and straining and misses the delicate way (the fan and the plug); the intellectual-bound goes for idealism and the exotic and lacks the efficiency and actual seeing into realities.

When insubstantiality and substantiality are not set and defined, when there is no track of changing, one has mastered the formless form. When there is a clinging to form, when there is attachment of the mind, it is not the true path. When technique comes out of itself, it is the Way growing out of no way.

The Immovable Mind
Do not be overconscious in sparring, or else you will be tied down—one would rather teach them to advance one step than to think of retreating one step.

The Five Main Points
1. The highest truth is inexpressible.
2. Spiritual cultivation cannot be cultivated.
3. In the last resort nothing is gained.
4. There is nothing much in the teaching.
5. In throwing punches and moving, therein lies the wonderful Tao.

Leaving sagehood behind and entering once more into ordinary humanity.

After coming to understand the other side, you come back and live on this side.

After the completion of cultivation (of no cultivation), one's thoughts continue to be detached from phenomenal things, and one still remains amid the phenomenal yet devoid of the phenomenal.

When both the man and his surroundings are eliminated—neither the man nor his surroundings are eliminated—WALK ON!

THE THEME

Basically this is a story of one man's quest for his liberation, the returning to his original sense of freedom. Unlike the Old West's "fastest gun alive," the individual is not out to sharpen his tools to destroy his antagonist; rather, his side kick, back fist, hook kick, and so forth, are directed primarily toward himself.

It is because of the self that there arises the foe. When there are no signs (or thought movements) stirred in your mind, no conflicts of opposition take place there; and where there are no conflicts (of one trying to "get the better" of the other), this is known as "neither self nor foe." At their best, the "tools" thus represent the force of intuitive or instinctive directness, which unlike the intellect, does not divide itself, blocking its own passageway. It marches onward without looking forward or sideways.

The basic problem of a martial artist is known as "psychical stoppage." This occurs when he is engaged in a deadly contest with his antagonist, and his mind attaches itself to thoughts or any object it encounters. Unlike the fluid mind in everyday life, his mind is "stopped," incapable of flowing from one object to another without stickiness or clogginess. At this point, the martial artist ceases to be master of himself, and, as a result, his tools no longer express themselves in their suchness. So to have something in one's mind means that it is preoccupied and has no time for anything else; however, to attempt to remove the thought already in it is to refill it with another something!

Source: Bruce Lee's handwritten note entitled "The Theme," from his notes for *The Silent Flute*, May 1970. Bruce Lee Papers.

Artist of Life

Ultimately, one should be "purposeless." By "purposeless" is not meant mere absence of things where vacant nothingness prevails. The object is not to be stuck with thought process. The spirit is by nature formless, and no "objects" are to be stuck in it. When anything is stuck there, your psychic energy loses its balance; its native activity becomes cramped and no longer flows with the stream. Where the energy is tipped, there is too much of it in one direction, while in another there is a shortage. Where there is too much, it overflows and cannot be controlled; where there is a shortage, it is not sufficiently nourished and shrivels up. In both cases, it is unable to cope with ever-changing situations.

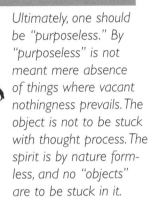

Ultimately, one should be "purposeless." By "purposeless" is not meant mere absence of things where vacant nothingness prevails. The object is not to be stuck with thought process. The spirit is by nature formless, and no "objects" are to be stuck in it.

But when there prevails a state of "purposelessness" (which is also a state of fluidity, empty-mindedness, or simply the everyday mind), the spirit harbors nothing in it, nor is it tipped in any one direction; it transcends both subject and object; it responds empty-mindedly to environmental changes and leaves no track. In Chuang-tzu's words: "The perfect man employs his mind as a mirror—it grasps nothing, yet it refuses nothing; it receives, but does not keep." Like water filling a pond, which is always ready to flow off again, the spirit can work its inexhaustible power because it is free and is open to everything because it is empty.

TRUE MASTERY

Three swordsmen sat down at a table in a crowded Japanese inn and began to make loud comments about their neighbor, hoping to goad him into a duel. The master seemed to take no notice of them, but when their remarks became ruder and more pointed, he raised his chopsticks and, in quick snips, effortlessly caught four flies on the wing. As he slowly laid down the chopsticks, the three swordsmen hurriedly left the room.

This story illustrates a great difference between Oriental and Western thinking. The average Westerner would be intrigued by someone's ability to catch flies with chopsticks, and would probably say that has nothing to do with how

To the Westerner, the finger jabs, the side kicks, the back fist and so forth, are tools of destruction and violence, which, indeed, are a couple of their functions. But the Oriental believes that the primary function of such tools is revealed when they are self-directed and destroy greed, fear, anger, and folly.

good he is in combat. But the Oriental would realize that a man who has attained such complete mastery of an art reveals his presence of mind in every action. The state of wholeness and imperturbability demonstrated by the master indicated his mastery of self.

And so it is with martial arts. To the Westerner, the finger jabs, the side kicks, the back fist, and so forth, are tools of destruction and violence, which, indeed, are a couple of their functions. But the Oriental believes that the primary function of such tools is revealed when they are self-directed and destroy greed, fear, anger, and folly.

Manipulative skill is not the Oriental's goal. He is aiming his kicks and blows at himself, and when successful, he may even succeed in knocking himself out. After years of training, he hopes to achieve that vital loosening and equability of all powers, which is what the three swordsmen saw in the master.

Source: Bruce Lee's handwritten Foreword to his personal copy of the script of *The Silent Flute*, October 19, 1970. Bruce Lee Papers.

In everyday life the mind is capable of moving from one thought or object to another—"being" mind instead of "having" mind. However, when one is face to face with an opponent in a deadly contest, the mind tends to stick and loses its mobility. Stick-ability or stoppage is a problem that haunts every martial artist.

Kwan-yin (Avalokitesvara), the Goddess of Mercy, is sometimes represented with one thousand arms, each holding a different instrument. If her mind stops with the use, for instance, of a spear, all the other arms (999) will be of no use whatever. It is only because of her mind not stopping with the use of one arm, but moving from one instrument to another, that all her arms prove useful with the utmost degree of efficiency. Thus this figure is meant to demonstrate that when the ultimate truth is realized, even as many as one thousand arms on one body may each be serviceable in one way or another.

"Purposelessness," "empty-mindedness," or "no art" are frequent terms used in the Orient to denote the ultimate achievement of a martial artist. According to Zen, the spirit is by nature formless, and no "objects" are to be harbored in it. When anything is harbored there, psychic energy loses its balance, its native activity becomes cramped, and it no longer flows with the stream. Where the energy is tipped, there is too much of it in one direction and a shortage of it in another direction. Where there is too much energy, it overflows and cannot be controlled. In either case, it is unable to cope with ever-changing situations. But when there prevails a state of "purposelessness" (which is also a state of fluidity or mindless-ness), the spirit harbors nothing in it, nor is it tipped in one direction. It transcends both subject and object; it responds with an empty-mind to whatever is happening.

True mastery transcends any particular art. It stems from mastery of oneself—the ability, developed through self-discipline, to be calm, fully aware, and completely in tune with oneself and the surroundings. Then, and only then, can a person know himself.

5-P
MARTIAL ART

Martial art, like any art, is an expression of the human being. Some expressions have taste, some are logical (maybe under certain required situations), but most involve merely performing some sort of a mechanical repetition of a fixed pattern.

This is most unhealthy because to live is to express, and to express you have to create. Creation is never something old, and definitely not merely repetition. Remember well my friend that all styles are man-made, and the man is always more important than any style. Style concludes. Man grows.

So martial art is ultimately an athletic expression of the dynamic human body. More important yet is the person who is there expressing his own soul. Yes, martial art is an unfolding of what a person is—his anger, his fears—and yet under all these natural human tendencies, which we all experience, after all, a "quality" martial artist can—in the midst of all these commotions—still be himself.

And it is not a question of winning or losing, but it is a question of being what is at that moment and being wholeheartedly involved with that particular moment and doing one's best. The consequence is left to whatever will happen.

Therefore to be a martial artist also means to be an artist of life. Since life is an ever-going process, one should flow in this process and discover how to actualize and expand oneself.

Source: Bruce Lee's handwritten essay, untitled. Bruce Lee Papers.

Artist of Life

OBSTACLES IN THE WAY OF KNOWLEDGE

In the long history of martial art, the instinct to follow and imitate seems to be inherent in most martial artists, instructor and student alike. This can be due partly to being human, and partly because of the patterns of styles (consequently finding a refreshing, original Master teacher is a rarity nowadays). Ever since the establishment of institutes, academies, schools, kwoons and their stylized instructors, the need for a "pointer of the Way" is echoed.

Each man belongs to a style that claims to possess truth to the exclusion of all other styles, and these styles become institutes with their explanations of the Way, dissecting and isolating the harmony of firmness and gentleness, establishing rhythmic forms as the encyclopedia of their particular techniques.

All goals, apart from the means, are therefore an illusion, and becoming is a denial of being. By an error repeated throughout the ages, truth, becoming a law or a faith, places obstacles in the way of knowledge. Method, which is in its very substance ignorance, encloses "truth" within a vicious circle. We should break such circles not by seeking knowledge, but by discovering the cause of ignorance.

Source: Bruce Lee's handwritten essay, undated. Bruce Lee Papers.

AN OBJECTIVE EVALUATION OF THE COMBATIVE SKILL OF BRUCE LEE

BY THOSE WHO KNOW WHAT IT IS

Ever since *The Big Boss*[27] there seems to be a wave, a hot wave in fact, of finding "another Bruce Lee" among all types of people, particularly martial artists. Ranging from karate men, hapkido men, judo men, and so forth, and so on. Forgetting about whether or not they possess the ability to act, just so as they can

kick or punch halfway decent and know a few tricks or gimmicks, the producers will make them a "star."

Now let's stop about here. Is it that simple to become a star? Well, I can assure you it's not that simple. Also, I can tell you that as more [of] Bruce Lee's films are shown, the audience will soon realize not only in acting ability, but in physical skill as well— they will see the difference. For example, in *The Way of the Dragon*, Bruce Lee's skill is matched with [that of] an American champion, Chuck Norris, who happens to be a seven-time winner of both the Ail-American Open and the World Karate Championship. Then there is Bob Wall, the 1970 Heavyweight Karate Champion, plus Wong In Sik, the seventh-degree hapkido expert, and some audiences may have seen him in the film called *Hapkido*.

Source: a never before published article, dictated on audiocassette by Bruce Lee entitled "An Objective Evaluation of the Combative Skill of Bruce Lee by Those Who Know What It Is," recorded in 1972, Hong Kong. Bruce Lee Archive.

"Of course, it is only movie-making," people will say. But I'm sure that the audiences are not so insensitive as to not be able to see and judge by themselves and compare the speed, power, rhythm, coordination, versatility, and so forth, of these men.

Black Belt magazine, the world's largest and a well-respected martial art magazine, has featured quite a few magazine articles on Bruce Lee [written] before he became an actor. I must emphasize here that *Black Belt* is a sort of a standard of what the international [martial arts] scene is all about—a quality and authoritative magazine. In an exclusive *Black Belt* interview survey done not too long ago, some opinions [were] expressed directly or indirectly by martial arts experts about the fighting ability of Bruce Lee.

Ernest Lieb

Ernest Lieb is a fifth-degree black belt (karate) and the director of the American Karate Association in the United States. He has this to say about Bruce Lee: "I have met Mr. Lee and have had the privilege of working out with him several times. Although I have won forty-two karate tournaments, I do not consider myself a match for him. His speed surpasses most of the black belts I know."

Jhoon Rhee

Jhoon Rhee, a seventh-degree black belt in tae kwon do, who is generally regarded as the man who introduced the Korean art of tae kwon do to America, describes Bruce's jeet kune do as "very scientific and practical, especially in street situations."

Chuck Norris

Chuck Norris, the American karate champion who recently did a movie with Bruce called *The All Way of the Dragon,* readily admitted to millions of people watching TV in a recent interview in Hong Kong that Bruce was his "teacher," and he considers him to be "fantastic." I must also add here that, at the same time, two other champions in karate—the heavyweight champion Joe Lewis and the light heavyweight champion Mike Stone, have, along with Chuck, been taking lessons from Bruce. Now all three of these men are from different styles and all are well established. Yet they come to learn under Bruce. In the Sport Week section of the *Washington*

Star, printed in Washington, D.C. on August 16, 1970, the following was written:

> Three of Bruce Lee's pupils, Joe Lewis, Chuck Norris, and Mike Stone, have between them won every major karate tournament in the United States. Joe Lewis was Grand National Champion three successive years. Bruce Lee handles and instructs these guys almost as a parent would a young child. Which can be somewhat disconcerting to watch. It's like walking into a saloon in the Old West and seeing the fastest guy in the territory standing there with notches all over his gun. Then in walks a pleasant little fellow who says 'How many times do I have to tell you? You're doing it all wrong!' And the other guy listens. Intently.

Ken Knudson

Ken Knudson, a powerful goju shorei stylist, a winner of many tournaments, says: "The power from Bruce's kicks and punches is bursting. He demonstrated a side kick on me that moved me so fast that I felt as though my eyeballs were still where I was standing when he kicked me. He uses logic, and I mean good logic, on all of his techniques." Ken is one of the top karatemen in the United States today.

Fred Wren

Fred Wren, another of the top ten karatemen in America, has nothing but praise for Bruce Lee. To put it in his own words in the survey, "I have never met anybody with more ability in fighting and knowledge than Mr. Lee himself."

Allen Steen

Allen Steen, winner of the Long Beach karate championship, is a two-hundred-pound six footer from Texas, and all he says is that "the parts of his [Bruce Lee's] art that he has shown me impress me greatly.

Wally Jay

Wally Jay, fifth-degree black belt holder in judo as well as Judo Coach of the Year in America, has [many] successful judo teams. He knows what constitutes a champion and a good competitor. He has this to say about Bruce: "Bruce is colorful, fascinating, and incomparable." Mr. Jay goes on to saying that he is "constantly amazed how Bruce can maintain his lightning speed without sacrificing his tremendous punching power." Wally has been in the martial art for over forty years. He compares Bruce "with the grace and the agility and the power of a black panther."

Louis Delgado

Louis Delgado, who's a black belt holder and who once beat Chuck Norris for the Grand Championship in New York, describes Bruce Lee in the November 1969 issue of *Black Belt* magazine as follows: "I have never seen anyone like Bruce Lee. I have met and sparred with several karate men, but Bruce has been the only one who has baffled me completely. I am completely in awe when I fight with him."

Jay Mather

In an open letter announcing the forthcoming karate winter championships, Jay Mather, the tournament holder who is also a black belt holder, describes Bruce's ability as having "made him a legend in his own time."

Hayward Nishioka

Hayward Nishioka, the Japanese-American National Judo champion, is also a black belt holder in the shotokan style of karate. Hayward ran a scientific test in a California university to find out the difference between a karate punch and a jeet kune do punch. And the finding was that, indeed, the jeet kune do punch is more powerful and destructive than the classical karate punch.

Joe Lewis

One thing worth mentioning here that is quite interesting (though I am aware that the Hong Kong martial arts circle is not so familiar with the American martial arts circle) is the encounter between Bruce Lee and the undisputed heavyweight karate champion, Joe Lewis. From what I gather, deep down inside Joe Lewis lies a deep respect of what Bruce knows and his ability to perform.

In case you don't know about Joe Lewis's image in the martial arts circles in America, he is kind of like the "bad boy" of karate. Many people look upon him as a bully. Well, he did break a few ribs; in fact, when Bob Wall, one of his students, who also appeared in Bruce's *The Way of the Dragon*, first met Joe in a freestyle sparring, three of Bob's ribs were broken by a side kick by Joe Lewis. Although Joe is egotistical and cocky by nature, he is good at what he is doing. According to *Black Belt* magazine's 1968 Yearbook, in which they reported on Lewis's win at the National Karate Tournament in Washington, D.C.:

Here, Lewis was in rare form and apparently reborn with a new technique, incorporating jeet kune do, and an ambition to conquer any opposition to his third straight karate championship in this arena. His usually surly disposition was put away in mothballs, so it seemed for this tourney and he was in general good spirits throughout, no doubt sparked by his sifu, Bruce Lee, who took extraordinary pride in his product. Lewis moved in and out of the battle with agility never seen before, and he pounded away at the opposition with such high caliber that the runners-up seemed faint shadows against the Lewis in evidence here. When Lewis was awarded the crown, he humbly thanked his sifu, Bruce Lee, giving him the credit for his improvement. Something Lewis had never done before! It looked like a new Lewis on the mat.

In case you have missed the recent news, Bruce Lee's jeet kune do—of which he is the founder—has been elected and accepted into the Black Belt Hall of Fame in America. This marks the first time a recently developed form of martial art has been accepted nationally. No, jeet kune do is not thousands or even hundreds of years old. It was started around 1965 by a dedicated and intensified man called Bruce Lee. And his martial art is something that no serious martial artist can ignore. And along with his skill and wisdom, there lies a real man, and I can only proudly say that he is one of us; our representative of what Chinese martial art is all about. Which, incidentally, ends our article right here.

Part 6

ACTING

Much like his attitude toward martial art, Lee regarded acting as an expression of one's self, referring to it as "the music of the soul made visible." It is not as widely known that Lee was an actor before he was a martial artist, having made eighteen Chinese-language pictures in Hong Kong before he reached the age of eighteen.

Acting was something that Lee was exposed to at a very early age. His father, Lee Hoi Chuen, was a very famous actor in the Cantonese Opera, so many of Lee's family friends were and remained actors.

Acting was an art form that continued to hold Lee's fascination throughout his lifetime. Even after he had effectively "made it" in the business, having become the hottest film property in the world by 1973, he was still purchasing books on the art and craft of acting and filmmaking in an effort to continue broadening his understanding and ability to become what he termed an "efficient deliverer."

These essays were drafted after Lee had returned to make films in Hong Kong between 1971 and 1973. Exact dates are not available, as Lee did not indicate them on his drafts. Nevertheless, they reveal a mind keenly devoted to intellectual and professional honesty and integrity, and the result was ultimately a very beautiful and successful "marriage" of business and art.

Artist of Life

WHAT EXACTLY IS AN ACTOR?

As far as I am concerned—and this is only my personal opinion—an actor is, first of all, like you and me, strictly a human being, and not a glamorous symbol known as a "star," which, after all, is an abstract word, a title given to you by people.

If you believe and enjoy all those flatteries (yes, we are only human, and we all do to a certain extent) and forget the fact that the same people who once were your "pals" might just desert you to make friends with another "winner" the moment you no longer are a winner, well, it's your choice. You own your right (although choice requires some self-inquiry here, it is still your choice; you have that right).

My more than twenty years' experience as an actor has caused me to look at it thusly: an actor is a dedicated being who works very hard—so damn hard that his level of understanding makes him a qualified artist in self-expression, physically, psychologically, as well as spiritually, to captivate.

Many of you know that I am a martial artist by choice, an actor by profession, and, by daily actualizing my potentiality through soulful discoveries and daily exercising (in my case) I hope to become also an artist of life.

Source: Bruce Lee's handwritten notes entitled "What Is an Actor?" Bruce Lee Papers.

AN ACTOR: THE SUM TOTAL

Depending on one's level of understanding, the movie industry nowadays is basically a coexistence of practical business sense and creative talent, each being the cause and the effect of the other.

To the administrators up in their administrative offices, an actor is a commodity, a product, a matter of money, money, money. "Whether or not it sells" is their chief concern. The important thing is the box-office appeal. In a way they are wrong, yet in a way they are right. I will go into that later. Although cinema is in fact a marriage of practical business and creative talent, but to regard an actor—a human being—as a product is somewhat emotionally aggravating to me.

An actor, a good actor, not the cliche type, is in reality a "competent deliverer," one who is not just ready but artistically harmonizes this invisible duality of business and art into a successful, appropriate unity. Mediocre actors, or cliche actors, are plentiful, but to settle down to train a "competent" actor mentally and physically is definitely not an easy task. Just as no two human beings are alike, so too with actors.

An actor, a good actor, not the cliche type, is in reality a "competent deliverer," one who is not just ready but artistically harmonizes this invisible duality of business and art into a successful, appropriate unity.

Source: Bruce Lee's handwritten notes on acting, untitled. Bruce Lee Papers.

A really trained, good actor is a rarity nowadays—that demands the actor to be real, to be himself. The audiences are not dumb today; an actor is not simply demonstrating what he wants others to believe he is expressing. That is mere imitation or illustration but it is not creating, even though this superficial demonstration can be "performed" with remarkable expertise.

Just what, then, is an actor of quality? To begin with, he is no "movie star," which is nothing but an abstract word given by the people, and a symbol. There are more people who want to become "movie stars" than [people who want to become] actors. To me, an actor is the sum total of all that he is—his high level of understanding of life, his appropriate good taste, his experience of happiness and adversities, his intensity, his educational background, and much, much more— like I said, the sum total of all that he is.

One more ingredient is that an actor has to be real in expressing himself as he would honestly in a given situation. An actor's problem, though, is not to be egotistical and to keep his cool and to learn more through discoveries and much deep soul-searching. Dedication, absolute dedication, is what keeps one ahead.

An actor's problem, though, is not to be egotistical and to keep his cool and to learn more through discoveries and much deep soul-searching. Dedication, absolute dedication, is what keeps one ahead.

6-B

SELF-ACTUALIZATION AND SELF-IMAGE ACTUALIZATION IN THE ART OF ACTING

The movie industry is sort of a mutual dependency between practical business sense and creative talent, although the former seems to be the trend. It is to be hoped that the actors or actresses are in reality "deliverers," so to sneak, so they can harmonize the duality of business and art into a form of successful, appropriate unity.

It is to be hoped that the actors or actresses are in reality "deliverers," so to speak, so they can harmonize the duality of business and art into a form of successful, appropriate unity.

It is definitely not difficult to get mediocre performers. As in the combative arts, to train a deliverer and make him ready, mentally and physically, is difficult enough, and to find one with just that right appropriateness and that rare quality of a dedicated artist can happen once in a blue moon.

Just what is an actor? Is he not the sum total of all understanding, his capability to captivate the audience because he is real in the expression of his personal feelings toward what is required by the scene. You can spot such

Just what is an actor? Is he not the sum total of all that he is? His level of understanding, his capability to captivate the audience because he is real in the expression of his personal feelings toward what is required by the scene.

artists from ordinary ones like that. The American has a word for it, it's called "charisma." What you see on the screen is the sum total of his level of understanding, his taste, his educational background, his intensity, and so forth, and so on.

Source: Bruce Lee's handwritten notes entitled "Self-Actualization and Self-image Actualization in the Art of Acting." Bruce Lee Papers.

ANOTHER ACTOR SPEAKS HIS MIND

This article expresses my personal true belief, a sort of personal view of the motion picture industry and the personal true belief of an actor as well as a human being. Above all, I have to take responsibility for myself and to do whatever is right. The script has to be right, the director has to be right, my time devoted toward preparation of the role. After that comes the money.

Now, to the business people in films (and I have to say cinema is a marriage of art and business), the actor is not a human being but a product, a commodity. However, you, as a human being, have the right to be the best goddamn product that ever walked and work so hard that the business people have to listen to you. You have that personal obligation to yourself to make yourself the best product possible according to your own terms. Not the biggest or the most successful, but the best quality—with that achieved, comes everything else.

A so-called "big star" doesn't necessarily mean a quality actor or actress. Indeed, the trouble is there exist too many people wanting to be stars rather than actors. That status symbol, a word that spells naiveness, that of liking to hear only what one wants to hear and actually believing that those "hangers on" will still be the "yes men" when that star suddenly becomes a worthless product; a non-salable commodity.

Source: Bruce Lee's handwritten personal essay entitled "Another Actor Speaks His Mind," Hong Kong, circa 1973. Bruce Lee Papers.

Part 7

SELF-KNOWLEDGE

Bruce Lee once wrote that "all types of knowledge ultimately mean self-knowledge," and, certainly, the need to know yourself was one of the dominant themes of Lee's teachings— particularly during the last four years of his life. Hollywood superstar Steve McQueen, who was a close friend of Lee's, once made this statement: "[Bruce] was very much into finding out who he was. His comment to people was 'know yourself, ... The good head that he acquired was through his knowing himself. He and I used to

have great long discussions about that. No matter what you do in life, if you don't know yourself, you're never going to be able to appreciate anything in life."[28]

This section presents Lee's beliefs—as he saw fit to commit them to paper—in regard to self-knowledge. The various drafts of "In My Own Process" harken back to his research into the psychology under- lying self-actualization—as opposed to self-image actualization. This was not merely academic posturing by Lee, but a key insight into the ultimate reality of what it means to be a human being. These essays are unquestionably the most revealing and compelling documents ever drafted by Bruce Lee.

THE FIRST ARTICLE I WRITE IN HONG KONG

This is the first article I am going to write about me, myself. It is not the usual goings on. Yet at this moment I am wondering for whom I'm writing this "organized mess." I have to say I am writing whatever wants to be written. Also included in these feelings [is] an urge to be as honest as I can—oh, I know, I am not being summoned by the court to tell the whole truth and nothing but the truth.

The undeniable fact is I am becoming a public figure. From a capable Chinese boxer—I'm no strategist, and if you call me vain, I try not to complain (you have your right)—suddenly I am a known actor. Mind you, actor, not star—I've gone through that, too. The sad fact is [that there are] too many people here wanting to be stars rather than quality actors or actresses.

I feel best when I am showing my skill off to the audience. Why? Because, baby, I have worked my X off to be able to do just that, and that means dedication, constant hard work, constant learning and discovering, plus lots of sacrifices.

Source: Bruce Lee's handwritten essay, untitled, circa 1973. Bruce Lee Papers.

IN MY OWN PROCESS: I

To begin with, this article is not an easy one because it is most difficult to write about oneself, because each of us is such a complexity. It is similar to an eye that can see externally but not internally. Granted, it would be a much easier job if one happens to be the type who can indulge oneself in a manipulative game of an imaginative self. But this bothers me.

I have come to the realization that sooner or later what it really amounts to is the bare fact that even an attempt to really write something about oneself demands, first of all, an honesty toward oneself, to be able to take responsibility to be what we actually are; that is, a pure human being.

Well, ever since I was a kid I have possessed within myself this instinctive urge for growth and daily expansion of my potential. It has been quite some time now since I acquired and really understood the dis-  *The truth is that life is an ever-going process, ever-renewing, and it is just meant to "lived," but not "lived for." It is something that cannot be squeezed into a self-constructed security pattern, a game of rigid control and clever manipulation.*

tinction between self-actualization and this illusion of self-image actualization. Through my own observations, I am convinced that an absolutely honest and direct inquiry into oneself will lead to understanding.

Source: Bruce Lee's handwritten essay entitled "In My Own Process,"

Artist of Life

The truth is that life is an ever-going process, ever-renewing, and it is just meant to "lived," but not "lived for." It is something that cannot be squeezed into a self-constructed security pattern, a game of rigid control and clever manipulation. Instead, to be what I term a "quality" human being one has to be transparently real and have the courage to be what he is.

Yet most people are doing just the opposite; they engage in a protective daily routine of security (a kind of thumb-sucking) by seeing themselves into some sort of various self-constructed, secured routine pattern in a rigid game.

Having gone through a lot of these ups and downs, I realize that there is no help but self-help. Self-help comes in many forms: daily discoveries through choiceless observation, honestly, as well as wholeheartedly always doing one's best; a sort of indomitable, obsessive dedication; and, above all, realizing that there is no end or limit to this, because life is simply an ever-going process, an ever-renewing process. The duty of a human being, in my personal opinion, is to become transparently real, to simply be.

In this world there are a lot of people who cannot touch the heart of the matter but talk merely intellectually (not emotionally) about how they would do this and that. [They] talk about it, but yet nothing is either actualized or accomplished. Of course, we have many others, and we can go into a few. Another type represents the "you should" be this, you SHOULD change that. A case of what should (a crystallized something) versus what is.

You can well say that I do not have any style, though I have to admit that I initiate from my wing chun instructor, Mr. Yip Man. We had tea not too long ago, and although our ideas differ, I respect this instructor of mine. Whatever happens, he is my wing chun instructor.

What it boils down to is my sincere and honest revelation of a man called Bruce Lee—that is, regarding his martial art (which always comes first), his viewpoint on movie-making, and last, but not least, just who is Bruce Lee? Where is he heading? What [does] he hope to discover?

To do this a person has to stand on his own two feet and find out his cause of ignorance. For the lazy and hopeless, they can forget it and do what they like best.

Artist of Life

7-C

IN MY OWN PROCESS: II

I don't know what I will be writing but just simply writing whatever wants to be written. If the writing communicates and stirs something within someone, it's beautiful. If not, well, it can't be helped.

Among people, great majorities don't feel comfortable at all with the unknown, that is, anything foreign that threatens their protected daily mold. So for the sake of their sense of security they construct chosen patterns, which they can justify.

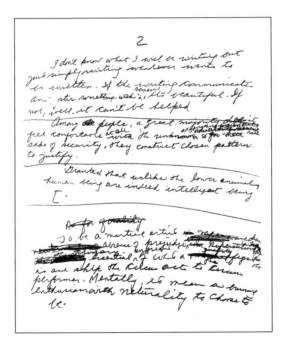

Granted, unlike the lower animals, human beings are indeed intelligent beings. To be a martial artist means and demands absence of prejudice, superstition, ignorance, and all that—the primary, essential ingredient of what a quality fighter is, and leave the circus acts to the circus performers. Mentally, it means a burning enthusiasm with neutrality to choose to be.

Source: Bruce Lee's handwritten note, untitled. Bruce Lee Papers.

IN MY OWN PROCESS: III

This article will include my own views on martial arts as well as acting and about life in general. Of course I will write what random thoughts keep popping up during the course, plus what I feel about writing this article at the moment, which I feel has the potential for good communication, so here goes. I am sure most people dislike the unknown and will think that, unlike the lower animals, we are indeed intelligent beings.

However, the problem is one where some people have a self, but most people have a void, because they are too busy wasting their vital creative energy to project themselves as this or that—dedicating their lives to actualizing a concept of what they should be like rather than actualizing their ever-growing potentiality as a human being; a sort of "being" versus having—that is, we do not "have" mind, we simply "are" mind. We are what we are.

Once the intelligence issue is established, I wonder how many of us have really gone to the trouble of reexamining all these so-called ready-made intelligent answers that are constantly crammed down our throats ever since heaven knows how long. Maybe starting from our first sign of capacity to learn. Yes, we possess a pair of eyes, the function of which is to observe, to discover, and so forth. Yet many of us simply do not really see in the true sense of the word. I must say that when the eyes are used externally to observe the inevitable faults of other beings, most of us are rather quick with ready-made condemnation.

For it is easy to criticize and break down the spirit of others, but to know yourself takes maybe a lifetime. To take responsibility for one's actions, good and bad, is something else. After all, all knowledge simply means self-knowledge.

Source: Bruce Lee's handwritten note, untitled. Bruce Lee Papers.

Self-knowledge

7-E

IN SEARCH OF SOMEONE REAL (IN MY OWN PROCESS: IV)

What the hell, you are what you are, and self-honesty occupies a definite and vital part in the ever-growing process to become a "real" human being and not a plastic one.

Ever since I was a kid, the word *quality* has meant a lot to me. Somehow I know and am devoting myself sincerely to it with much sacrifice and heading toward a direction, and you can rest assured that Mr. Quality himself will always be there. Somehow, one day, you will hear, "Hey, now that's quality. Here is someone REAL." I'd like that.

In life, what can you ask for but to be real; to fulfill your potential instead of wasting energy on actualizing your dissipating image, which is not real and means expending your vital energy. We have great work ahead of us, and it requires devotion and much, much energy. To grow, to discover, we need involvement, which is something I experience every day, sometimes good, sometimes frustrating. No matter what, you must let your Inner Light guide you out of the darkness.

I have to say I am writing what happens to be popping into my mind. It might be incoherent to some, but, what the heck, I don't care. I'm just simply writing whatever wants to be written at the moment of its conception. If we communicate, which I sincerely hope, it's cool. If not, well, it can't be helped anyway.

For those who want to know, I am a martial artist by choice, an actor by profession (which to me is an expressive revelation and/or learning of myself), and I am actualizing myself daily to be an artist of life as well. After all, all arts have a similar foundation! You are free to make your own choice of expressing your instinctive potentiality. Of course, what is your conception of "quality"? I will start with martial art, which is my first love.

For those who want to know, I am a martial artist by choice, an actor by profession (which to me is an expressive revelation and/or learning of myself), and I am actualizing myself daily to be an artist of life as well.

7-F

IN MY OWN PROCESS: V

Any attempt to write a "meaningful" article on anyone, that is, how he feels and thinks, is first of all, a very difficult assignment. To write about oneself, meaningfully, that is, is even worse. As though things aren't tough enough, I am in the midst of preparing a new movie, *Enter the Dragon*, a joint venture between Concord and Warner Brothers, plus another Concord production, *The Game of Death*, which is only halfway done. I have been busy, yet this article deserves my undivided attention at this moment. If somehow I can communicate with somebody, I am satisfied; if not, it cannot be helped.

Of course, this writing can be made less demanding should I allow myself to indulge in the standard manipulating game of role-playing, but my responsibility to myself disallows that. I am what I am here and now. Oh, I know, I am not called upon to write any true confession, but I do want to be honest; that is the least a human being can do, the one element of making this article meaningful.

I have always been a martial artist by choice, an actor by profession, but above all, [I] am actualizing myself to be an artist of life. Yes, there is a difference between self-actualization and self-image actualization.

Most people live only for their image; that is why whereas some have a self, a starting point, most people have a void, because they are so busy projecting themselves as this or that. Wasting, dissipating all their energy in projection and conjuring up a facade, rather than centering their energy on expanding and broadening their potential or expressing and relaying this unified energy for efficient communication, and so forth. When another human being sees a self-actualizing person walk past, he cannot help but say, "Hey, now there is someone real!"

Source: Bruce Lee's handwritten personal essay entitled "In My Own Process," circa 1973. Bruce Lee Papers.

Oh, I know we all admit that we are intelligent beings; yet I wonder how many of us have gone through some sort of self-inquiries and/or self-examining of all the ready-made facts or truths that are crammed down our throats ever since we acquired the capacity and the sensibility to learn.

Though we possess a pair of eyes, most of us do not really see in the true sense of the word. True seeing, in the sense of choiceless awareness, leads to new discovery, and discovery is one of the means to uncovering our potentiality. However, when this same pair of eyes is used to observe or discover other people's faults, we are quick with ready-made condemnation. For it is easy to criticize and break down the spirit of others, but to know yourself takes maybe a lifetime.

IN MY OWN PROCESS ------- BY BRUCE LEE.

Any attempt to write a "meaningful" article on anyone, that is, how he feels and thinks is first of all, a very difficult assignment. To write about oneself, meaningfully that is, is even worse. So though things aren't tough enough, I am in the midst of preparing a new movie "Enter The Dragon 龍爭虎鬥", a joint venture between Concord and Warner Brothers, plus another Concord production "The Game of Death", which is only half way done. I have been busy yet this Article deserves my undivided attention at the moment. If somehow I can communicate with somebody, I am satisfied; if not, it cannot be helped.

Of course, this writing can be made less demanding should I allow myself indulging in the standard manipulating game of role playing, but my responsibility to myself disallow that. I am what I am here and now. Oh I know, I am not called in to write any true confession, but I do want to be honest, that is the least a human being can do, some element of making this article meaingful.

I have always been a martial artist by choice, an actor by profession, but above all, am actualizing myself someday to be an artist of life. Yes, there is a difference between self-actualization and

IN MY OWN PROCESS: VI

Bruce Lee is a changing person because he is and always will be learning, discovering, and expanding. Like his martial art, his learnings are never fixed. They keep changing. At best, Bruce Lee presents a possible direction, but nothing more.

Some significant traits of Bruce Lee which the author finds admirable are his honesty to himself, quality over quantity (to put it in his words, "I can walk away from millions because it's not right, but I'll be damned if I'll back up an inch from a dime because it has to be so"). Last but not least, he is a hardworking man, although over 90 percent of the superstars who would be in his shoes would be neglecting his worth and would abuse his power.

Source: Bruce Lee's handwritten notes entitled "Notes on Article." Bruce Lee Papers.

IN MY OWN PROCESS: VII (ON SELF-ACTUALIZATION)

Ever since I was a kid I have [had] this instinctive urge and craving for expansion and growth. To me the function and duty of a human being, a quality human being, that is (here I don't include the group of people who don't quite know what life is all about), is the sincere and honest development of his potential and "self-actualization." Not self-image actualization. Though I have to interrupt here to say that at one time, quite a long time ago, I did get on the kick of self-image actualization rather than "self-actualization."

I have discovered another quality over the spread of a decade. I have long been in the process of discovering through earnest personal experiences and dedicated learning that ultimately the greatest help is self-help. That there is no other help but self-help, to honestly do one's best, dedicating oneself wholeheartedly to a given task, which happens to have no end but, rather, is an ongoing process.

I have done a lot during these years of my process. Well, in my process I have changed from self-image actualization to self-actualization, from blindly following propaganda, organized truths, and so forth, to searching internally for the cause of my ignorance. I am a hardworking man.

Source: Bruce Lee's handwritten personal essay, untitled, circa 1973. Bruce Lee Papers.

IN MY OWN PROCESS: VIII

Any attempt to write a "meaningful" article on how I, Bruce Lee, feel and think or express myself is, first of all, a very difficult task because I am still in the process of learning, constantly discovering and constantly growing.

As though this assignment is not tough enough, I am in the midst of preparing my next movie, *Enter the Dragon,* a production between Concord and Warner Bros., plus another Concord production, *The Game of Death,* which is only halfway done. I have been busy and occupied with mixed emotions as of late.

Of course, this writing could be made less demanding should I allow myself to indulge in the usual manipulating game of role creation. Fortunately for me, my self-knowledge has transcended that, and I've come to understand that life is best lived—not conceptualized.

I am happy because I am growing daily and honestly, and I don't know where my ultimate limit lies. To be certain, every day there can be a revelation or a new discovery that I can obtain. However, the most gratification is yet to come, to hear another human being say, "Hey, now here is something real!"

I am happy because I am growing daily and honestly, and I don't know where my ultimate limit lies. To be certain, every day there can be a revelation or a new discovery that I can obtain.

Oh, I know, I am not called upon to write any true confession, but I do want to be honest—that is the least a human being can do. Basically, I have always been a martial artist by choice, and actor by profession. But, above all, I am hoping to actualize myself to be an artist of life along the way.

Source: Bruce Lee's handwritten personal essay entitled "In My Own Process," circa 1973. Bruce Lee Papers.

By martial art, I mean, like any art, it is an unrestricted athletic expression of an individual soul. Oh yes, martial art also means daily hermitlike physical training to upgrade or maintain one's quality. However, martial art is also about the unfolding [of] the bare human soul. That is what interests me.

Yes, I have grown quite a bit since the day when I first became a martial artist, and I am still growing as I continue my process. To live is to express oneself freely in creation. Creation, I must say, is not a fixed something, a solidification.

So I hope my fellow martial artists would open up and be transparently real, and I wish them well in their own process of finding their cause.

THE PASSIONATE STATE OF MIND

We can see through others only when we see through ourselves.

Lack of self-awareness renders us transparent; a soul that knows itself is opaque.

It is compassion rather than the principle of justice that can guard us against being injurious to our fellow man.

We have more faith in what we imitate than in what we originate. We cannot derive a sense of absolute certitude from anything that has its roots in us. The most poignant sense of insecurity comes from standing alone; we are not alone when we imitate. It is thus with most of us! We are what other people say we are. We know ourselves chiefly by hearsay.

Our sense of power is more vivid when we break a man's spirit than when we win his heart. For we can win a man's heart one day and lose it the next. But when we break a proud spirit we achieve something that is final and absolute.

Fear comes from uncertainty. When we are absolutely certain, whether of our worth or worthlessness, we are almost impervious to fear. Thus a feeling of utter unworthiness can be a source of courage.

There is a powerful craving in most of us to see ourselves as instruments in the hands of others and thus free ourselves from the responsibility for acts that are prompted by our own questionable inclinations and impulses. Both the strong and the weak grasp at the alibi. The latter hide their malevolence under the virtue of obedience; they acted dishonorably because they had to obey orders. The strong, too, claim absolution by proclaiming themselves the chosen instrument of a higher power—God, history, fate, nation, or humanity.

Everything seems possible when we are absolutely helpless or absolutely powerful—and both states stimulate our credulity.

Source: Bruce Lee's handwritten essay entitled "The Passionate State of Mind." Bruce Lee Papers.

Pride is a sense of worth derived from something that is not organically part of us; while self-esteem derives from the potentialities and achievements of self. We are proud when we identify ourselves with an imaginary self, a leader, a holy cause, a collective body of possessions. There is fear and intolerance in pride; it is insensitive and uncompromising. The less promise and potency in the self, the more imperative is the need for pride. The core of pride is self-rejection. It is true that when pride releases energies and serves as a spur to achievement, it can lead to a reconciliation with the self and the attainment of genuine self-esteem.

We acquire a sense of worth either by realizing our talents, or by keeping busy, or by identifying ourselves with something apart from us—be it a cause, a leader, a group, possessions and the like. Of the three, the path of self-realization is the most difficult. It is taken only when other avenues to a sense of worth are more or less blocked. Men of talent have to be encouraged and goaded to engage in creative work. Their groans and laments echo through the ages.

Action is a high road to self-confidence and esteem. Where it is open, all energies flow toward it. It comes readily to most people and its rewards are tangible. The cultivation of the spirit is elusive and

The cultivation of the spirit is elusive and difficult, and the tendency toward it is rarely spontaneous. When the opportunities for action are many, cultural creativeness is likely to be neglected.

difficult, and the tendency toward it is rarely spontaneous. When the opportunities for action are many, cultural creativeness is likely to be neglected. The cultural flowering of New England came to an almost abrupt end with the opening of the West. The relative cultural sterility of the Romans might perhaps be explained by their Empire rather than by an innate lack of genius. The best talents were attracted by the rewards of administrative posts, just as the best talents in America are attracted by the rewards of a business career.

A fateful process is set in motion when the individual is released "to the freedom of his own impotence" and left to justify his existence by his own efforts. The autonomous individual, striving to realize himself and prove his worth, has created all that is great in literature, art, music, science, and technology. The autonomous individual, also, when he can neither realize himself nor justify his existence by his own efforts, is a breeding of frustration, and the seed of the convulsions that shake our world to its foundations. The individual on his own is stable only so long as he is possessed of self-esteem. The maintenance of self-esteem is a continuous task that taxes all of the individual's power and inner resources. We have to prove our worth and justify our existence anew each day. When, for whatever reason, self-esteem is unattainable, the autonomous individual becomes a highly explosive entity. He turns away from an unpromising self and plunges into the pursuit of pride—the explosive substitute for self-esteem. All social disturbances and upheavals have their roots in a crisis of individual self-esteem, and the great endeavors in which the masses most readily unite is basically a search for pride.

The propensity to action is symptomatic of an inner unbalance. To be balanced is to be more or less at rest. Action is at bottom a swinging and flailing of the arms to regain one's balance and keep afloat. And if it be true, as Napoleon wrote to Carnot, that "the art of government is not to let men grow stale," then it is an art of unbalancing. The crucial difference between a totalitarian regime and a free social order is perhaps in the methods of unbalancing by which the people are kept active and striving.

The propensity to action is symptomatic of an inner unbalance. To be balanced is to be more or less at rest. Action is at bottom a swinging and flailing of the arms to regain one's balance and keep afloat.

We are told that talent creates its own opportunities. But it sometimes seems that intense desire creates not only its own opportunities, but its own talents.

The times of drastic change are times of passion. We can never be fit and ready for that which is wholly new. We have to adjust ourselves, and every radical adjustment is a crisis in self-esteem: we undergo a test; we have to prove ourselves. A population subjected to drastic change is thus a population of misfits, and misfits

Artist of Life

live and breathe in an atmosphere of passion.

That we pursue something passionately does not always mean that we really want it or have a special aptitude for it. Often the thing we pursue most passionately is but a substitute for the one thing we really want and cannot have. It is usually safe to predict that the fulfillment of an excessively cherished desire is not likely to still our nagging anxiety. In every passionate pursuit, the pursuit counts more than the object pursued.

Humility is not renunciation of pride but the substitution of one pride for another.

It is doubtful whether there is such a thing as impulsive or natural tolerance. Tolerance requires an effort of thought and self-control. And acts of kindness, too, are rarely without deliberateness and "thoughtfulness." Thus it seems that some artificiality, some posing and pretense, are inseparable from any act or attitude that involves a limitation of our appetites and selfishness. We ought to beware of people who do not think it necessary to pretend that they are good and decent. Lack of hypocrisy in such things hints at a capacity for a most depraved ruthlessness. (Pretense is often an indispensable step in the attainment of genuineness. It is a form into which genuine inclinations flow and solidify.)

The control of our being is not unlike the combination of a safe. One turn of the knob rarely unlocks the safe. Each advance and retreat is a step toward one's goal.

Secretiveness can be a source of pride. It is a paradox that secretiveness plays the same role as boasting: in both we are engaged in the creation of a disguise. Boasting tries to create an imaginary self, while secretiveness gives us the exhilarating feeling of being princes disguised in meekness. Of the two, secretiveness is the more difficult and effective, for in the self-observant boasting breeds self-contempt. Yet it is as Spinoza said: "Men govern nothing with more difficulty than their tongues, and can moderate their desires more than their words."

To become different from what we are, we must have some awareness of what we are. Whether being different results in dissimulation or a real change of heart—it cannot be realized without self-awareness. Yet it is remarkable that the very people who are most self-dissatisfied and crave most for a new identity have the least self-awareness. They have turned away from an unwanted self and hence never had a good look at it. The result is that those most dissatisfied can neither dissimulate nor attain a real change of heart. They are transparent, and their unwanted qualities persist through all attempts at self-dramatization and self-transformation.

LETTERS

*Throughout his lifetime, Bruce Lee was a very prolific letter writer.
He would write to his friends frequently and often in considerable
depth in order to bring them up to date on new career developments
or philosophical/spiritual insights that had come to him.*

*The following letters are excerpted from Volume 5 of The Bruce
Lee Library Series,* Bruce Lee: Letters of the Dragon, *and serve as
snapshots of many of the points revealed in previous sections of this
book.*

*Each of these letters represents an aspect of Lee's philosophy,
psychology, poetry, self-help/self-knowledge, and martial art beliefs,
and together they further show how he was able to interface all of these
facets into his daily life.*

Artist of Life

8-A

"THE TRUE MEANING OF LIFE— PEACE OF MIND"

To Pearl Tso[29]

September 1962

Dear Pearl,
This letter is hard to understand. It contains my dreams and my ways of thinking. As a whole, you can call it my way of life. It will be rather confusing as it is difficult to write down exactly how I feel. Yet I want to write and let you know about it. I'll do my best to write it clearly and I hope that you, too, will keep an open mind in this letter, and don't arrive at any conclusions till you are finished.

There are two ways of making a good living. One is the result of hard work, and the other, the result of the imagination (requires work, too, of course). It is a fact that labor and thrift produce a competence, but fortune, in the sense of wealth, is the reward of the man who can think of something that hasn't been thought of before. In every industry, in every profession, ideas are what America is looking for. Ideas have made America what she is, and one good idea will make a man what he wants to be.

Source: Bruce Lee's handwritten letter to Pearl Tso, September 1962. Bruce Lee Papers.

One part of my life is gung fu. This art has been a great influence in the formation of my character and ideas. I practice gung fu as a physical culture, a form of mental training, a method of self-defense, and a way of life. Gung fu is the best of all martial art; yet the Chinese derivatives of judo and karate, which are only basics of gung fu, are flourishing all over the United States. This so happens because no one has [yet] heard of this supreme art; also there are no competent instructors. I believe my long years of practice back up my title to become the first instructor of this movement. There are yet long years ahead of me to polish my techniques and character. My aim, therefore, is to establish a first gung fu institute that will later spread out all over the United States (I have set a time limit of ten to fifteen years to complete the whole project).

My reason in doing this is not the sole objective of making money. The motives are many and among them are: I like to let the world know about the greatness of this Chinese art; I enjoy teaching and helping people; I would like to have a well-to-do home for my family; I like to originate something; and the last but yet one of the most important is because gung fu is part of myself.

I know my idea is right, and, therefore, the results would be satisfactory. I don't really worry about the reward, but to set in motion the machinery to achieve it. My contribution will be the measure of my reward and success.

Before he passed away, some asked the late Dr. Charles R. Steinmetz, the electrical genius, in his opinion "What branch of science would make the most progress in the next twenty-five years?" He paused and thought for several minutes then like a flash replied, "spiritual realization." When man comes to a conscious vital realization of those great spiritual forces within himself and begins to use those forces in science, in business, and in life, his progress in the future will be unparalleled.

I feel I have this great creative and spiritual force within me that is greater than faith, greater than ambition, greater than confidence, greater than determination, greater than vision. It is all these combined. My brain becomes magnetized with this dominating force which I hold in my hand.

When you drop a pebble into a pool of water, the pebble starts a series of ripples that expand until they encompass the whole pool.

This is exactly what will happen when I give my ideas a definite plan of action. Right now, I can project my thoughts into the future, I can see ahead of me. I dream (remember that practical dreamers never quit). I may now own nothing but a little place down in a basement, but once my imagination has got up a full head of steam, I can see painted on a canvas of my mind a picture of a fine, big five- or six-story gung fu institute with branches all over the States. I am not easily discouraged, readily visualize myself as overcoming obstacles, winning out over setbacks, achieving "impossible" objectives.

Whether it is the God-head or not, I feel this great force, this untapped power, this dynamic something within me. This feeling defies description, and [there is] no experience with which this feeling may be compared. It is something like a strong emotion mixed with faith, but a lot stronger.

All in all, the goal of my planning and doing is to find the true meaning in life—peace of mind. I know that the sum of all the possessions I mentioned does not necessarily add up to peace of mind; however, it can if I devote myself to real accomplishment of self rather than neurotic combat. In order to achieve this peace of mind, the teaching of detachment of Taoism and Zen will prove to be valuable.

Probably, people will say I'm too conscious of success. Well, I am not. You see, my will to do springs from the knowledge that I CAN DO. I'm only being natural, for there is no fear or doubt inside my mind.

Pearl, success comes to those who become success-conscious. If you don't aim at an object, how the heck on earth do you think you can get it?

Warm regards,
Bruce

8-B

"USE YOUR OWN EXPERIENCE AND IMAGINATION"

To Taky Kimura[30]

Taky,

I've just rushed the T'ai Kik[31] wall chart form to you. Enclosed in the parcel was a Chinese jacket. As I've mentioned, I've just got back from Oakland, and James Lee is going to send you a Lop Sao apparatus with built-in resistance.

First and foremost, I would like to impress a most important rule of teaching in your mind, and that is the economy of form. Follow this rule and you will NEVER feel like you have to ADD more and more so-called "sizzling" techniques to keep your students interested.

Source: Bruce Lee's handwritten letter to Taky Kimura, circa 1965. Bruce Lee Papers.

In order to explain "Economy of Form," I'll take a technique to illustrate the theory. Later on this idea can be applied to any technique. Together with the idea of "The Three Stages of a Technique" ([1] synchronization of self, [2] synchronization with opponent, [3] under fighting condition) this program of teaching not only provides an endless routine of instruction, but a most efficient lesson plan that will bring results to ALL students. I've tested them here in LA and disregarding how LITTLE we show each time, the students' interest is kept up because they have to eliminate the extra motions involved, and they feel great doing it. All right, back to the idea of "ECONOMY OF FORM."

To illustrate the idea, I'll take the Pak Sao (slapping hand)—basically, "ECONOMY OF MOTION" means ALL motions start from the By-Jong position; secondly, HANDS ARE TO MOVE FIRST IF IT IS A HAND TECHNIQUE (FOOT FOLLOWS), FEET FIRST IF IT IS A FOOT TECHNIQUE.

So emphasize the above "Two Truths" by practicing Pak Sao first in the touching hand manner—in other words, students in Bai-Jong position touching each other's hand—though in real combat, one will never start by touching hand; however, this touching hand position will ensure correct form in the beginning stage—economy of form, that is.

Each student must attack [in unison] FROM THE BAI-JONG without any wasted motion. Now this has been an overlooked basic theory of utmost importance. If any student does his Pak Sao [or any technique for that matter] with wasted motion, back to the touching hand position he goes to MINIMIZE his unnecessary motions. So you see that in order to progress to apply Pak Sao from a distance, this touching hand position has to be mastered. Not only that, the student has to return to the touching hand position to remind him to eliminate unnecessary motion periodically.

From a distance, Pak Sao is a lot harder—without any given away motion, one must initiate first hand, then feet, in a progressive, harmonious forward motion—no wonder not too many can hit with a single Pak Sao! Do you not see now the idea of economy of motion? Just this one theory of economy of motion takes up one heck of a lot of time for perfection, not to mention the "Three Stages of a Technique"—that is, in terms of Pak Sao—and after learning and mastering Pak Sao from a distance, one has to bridge the gap between [one and one's] opponent with a kick—to close in safely.

Following the above suggestion will give you endless hours of instruction. Of course, you must use the set system, that is REPETITION of each technique in sets for perfection. You begin now immediately to work on what I mentioned and apply all you've learned with ECONOMY OF MOTION—you will double your speed and skill doing just that.

I hope I have impressed in your mind a most important rule of our style—stick to the program I've given you, use variety, and do not worry too much that your students need more and more to stay with you—true [only] if they can do perfectly all you've taught them.

Remember the idea that one has to come in thousands of times in order to perfect one judo throw. And, of course, use your own experience and imagination. You will do well.

I have faith in you,

Bruce

8-C

"WHO AM I?"

To Jhoon Goo Rhee[32]

Jhoon Goo,
Enclosed please find [Chuck] Norris's ad. This is the most recent one. I'll try to save them for you in the future. Also, I have included other ads of similar nature, which might be of help.

[Bruce Lee then included the following two poems, which he wrote to help encourage his old friend, advising him not to let circumstances adversely affect him and to realize that each individual is the captain of his own soul and the controller of his destiny.]

Source: Bruce Lee's handwritten letter to Jhoon Rhee. Jhoon Rhee Archives.

Who am I?

Who am I?
That is the age-old question
Asked by every man
At one time or another.

Though he looks into a mirror
And recognizes the face,
Though he knows his own name
And age and history,
Still he wonders, deep down,
Who am I?

Am I a giant among men,
Master of all I survey,
Or an ineffectual pygmy
Who clumsily blocks his own
     way?

Am I the self-assured
     gentleman
With a winning style,
The natural born leader
Who makes friends instantly,
Or the frightened heart
Tiptoeing among strangers,

Who, behind a frozen smile,
     trembles
Like a little boy lost in a dark
     forest?

Most of us yearn to be one,
But fear we are the other.
Yet we CAN be
What we aspire to be.

Those who cultivate
Their natural instincts,
Who set their sights
On the good, the admirable,
     the excellent,
Will find their confidence
     rewarded.

And, in the process,
They will discover the true
     identity
Of him who looks back from
     the mirror.

Which Are You?

The doubters said,
"Man cannot fly."
The doers said,
"Maybe, but we'll try,"
And finally soared
Into the morning's glow
While nonbelievers
Watched from below.

The doubters claimed
The world was flat.
Ships plunged over its edge,
And that was that!

Yet a brand new world
Some doers found,
And returned to prove
This planet round.

The doubters knew
'Twas fact, "Of course,
No noisy gadget
Would e'er replace the horse."

Yet the carriages
Of doers, sans equine,
Came to traverse
All our roads in time.

But [to] those who kept saying
"It can't be done,"
Never are the victories
Or the honors won.
But, rather,
By the believing, doing kind,
While the doubters
Watched from far behind.

In conclusion, may I warn you that negativeness very often unknowingly creeps up upon us. It helps occasionally to stop all thoughts (the chattering of worries, anticipations, and so forth, in your head) and then once more refreshingly march bravely on.

Just as the maintaining of good health may require the taking of unpleasant medicine, so the condition of being able to do the things we enjoy often requires the performance of a few we don't. Remember my friend that it is not what happens that counts; it is how you react to events.

You have what it takes. I know you will win out one way or the other. So damn the torpedo, full speed ahead! Remember what this Chinaman says, "Circumstances? Hell, I make circumstances!"

Peace and harmony,
Bruce

"TURNING STUMBLING BLOCKS INTO STEPPING STONES"

To Jhoon Rhee

Jhoon Goo,

Greetings from Los Angeles where, like many places in the States, business is not too good. Don't misunderstand me that this is a pessimistic statement, though the fact is just as it is, but like anybody else, you have your choice of reacting to it. Here I ask you, Jhoon Goo, are you going to make your obstacles stepping stones to your dreams, or stumbling blocks because unknowingly you let negativeness, worries, fear, and so forth, to take over you?

Believe me that in every big thing or achievement there [are] always obstacles, big or small, and the reaction one shows to such obstacles is what counts, not the obstacle itself. There is no such thing as defeat until you admit one to yourself, but not until then!

My friend, do think of the past in terms of those memories of events and accomplishments which were pleasant, rewarding, and satisfying. The present? Well, think of it in terms of challenges and opportunities, and the rewards available for the application of your talents and energies. As for the future, that is a time and a place where every worthy ambition you possess is within your grasp.

Source: Bruce Lee's handwritten letter to Jhoon Rhee. Jhoon Rhee Archives.

You have a tendency to waste a lot of your energy in worry and anticipation. Remember my friend to enjoy your planning as well as your accomplishment, for life it too short for negative energy.

Since the India trip my back is so-so. *Silent Flute* is still on with Warner Bros. We are waiting to hear the next step, and should know within ten days—approval of new budget, setting up another survey trip, and so forth. Aside from *Silent Flute*, I will do a guest appearance on a new TV series *Longstreet* for next season. Then there is another movie that I will do (one of the three leading characters) should the presentation be approved, and that we should know within ten days or so, too.

Of course, the damn thing is I want to do something now! So I have created a TV series idea and I should know within a couple of weeks. In the meantime, I am working on another idea for a movie to do in Hong Kong (Chinese movie). So action! Action! Never wasting energy on worries and negative thoughts. I mean who has the most insecure job as I have? What do I live on? My faith in my ability that I'll make it. Sure my back [injury] screwed me up good for a year but with every adversity comes a blessing because a shock acts as a reminder to oneself that we must not get stale in routine. Look at a rain storm; after its departure everything grows!

So remember that one who is possessed by worry not only lacks the poise to solve his own problems, but by his nervousness and irritability creates additional problems for those around him.

Well, what more can I say but damn that torpedo, full speed ahead!

From a martial artist with a screwed up back but who has discovered a new powerful kick!

Bruce Lee

"IT'S ALL IN THE STATE OF MIND"

To Larry Hartsell[33]

June 6, 1971

Dear Larry,

How's your hip? I hope you're taking care of yourself.

I'll be doing a TV show the end of this month. The show is called *Long-street,* a new TV series for this coming fall. The episode I'll be in is titled "The Way of the Intercepting Fist."

Nothing new developed with *Silent Flute*—it's a matter of time. Am in the process of creating a new TV series based on martial art, hope it will turn out—will let you know.

I'll be on the cover of the next issue of *Black Belt.* Read it, you might find it interesting.

I've never met your family but do give them my best regards.

Take care my friend,

Bruce Lee

Source: Bruce Lee's handwritten letter to Larry Hartsell, June 1971. Larry Hartsell Archives.

[Lee then enclosed one of his favorite motivational poems, one that praised the power of positive thinking in the face of adversity. It was enclosed as a motivational tool to strengthen his friend's will to recover.]

If you think you are beaten, you are.
If you think you dare not, you don't.
If you like to win, but think you can't
It is almost certain you won't.
If you think you will lose, you are lost.
For out of the world we find
Success BEGINS with a fellow's WILL.
It's all in the state of mind.
If you think you're outclassed, you are.
You've got to think high to rise.
You've got to be sure of yourself before
You can ever win a prize.
Life's battles don't always go to
The stronger or faster man.
But sooner or later the man
Who wins is the man
WHO THINKS HE CAN!

8-F

"ART LIVES WHERE ABSOLUTE FREEDOM IS"

To "John"[34]

Dear John,

You hit the nail right on the head. I've just been back from a dubbing session—busy is the word!

Sincerity seems to be part of your makeup and though we've not been together for too long, my immediate reply to you is as follows: (a) timewise I wouldn't have time to teach, but I'm willing—when time permits—to honestly express or "to open myself" to you, to act as sort of a sign pole for a traveler.

My experience will help, but I insist and maintain that art—true art, that is—cannot be handed out. Furthermore, art is never decoration or embellishment. Instead it is a constant process of maturING (in the sense of NOT having arrived!).

You see, John, when we have the opportunity of working out, you'll see that your way of thinking is definitely not the same as mine. Art, after all, is a means of acquiring "personal" liberty. Your way is not my way nor mine yours.

So whether or not we can get together, remember well that art "LIVES" where absolute freedom is. With all the training thrown to nowhere, with a mind (if there is such a verbal substance) perfectly unaware of its own working, with the "self" vanishing nowhere the art of JKD attains its perfection.

I have to hit the sack now 'cause I have to work early tomorrow plus training afterward. This is just a short note to a fellow martial artist.

"The process of becoming,"

Bruce

Source: Bruce Lee's handwritten letter to "John," circa 1972. Bruce Lee Papers.

Notes

Front Matter

1. Bruce Lee's handwritten essay entitled "In My Own Process," circa 1973. Bruce Lee Papers.
2. Bruce Lee quoted from an interview with Pierre Berton, published in *Bruce Lee: Words from a Master*, p. II, published by NTC/Contemporary Publishing Group, Inc., Chicago.
3. Ibid., p. 37.
4. Bruce Lee's handwritten notes entitled "Commentaries on the Martial Way," Volume I, circa 1970. Bruce Lee Papers.
5. Bruce Lee's handwritten letter to "John" is also published on page 167 of Volume 5 of *The Bruce Lee Library Series: Letters of the Dragon*, edited by John Little, published by the Charles E. Tuttle Publishing Company, Boston, (c) 1998 Linda Lee Cadwell.
6. Bruce Lee's handwritten annotation within his script from *Longstreet*, June 27, 1971. Bruce Lee Papers.

Main Text

1. L Adam Beck, *The Story of Oriental Philosophy*, 1928, N.Y.
2. L Frank N. Magill, *Masterpieces of World Philosophy* N.Y.
3. Huston Smith, *The World's Religions*, 1957.
4. *I'Ching*, translated Carry F. Baynes, 1960, N.Y
5. Lao-tzu, *The Way of Life*, translated by R. B. Blakney, 1955, N.Y.
6. Glenn Clark, *Power in Athletics*.
7. Alan Watts, *The Way of Zen*, 1957, N.Y.
8. *I'Chmg*, translated by Carry F. Baynes, 1960, N.Y.
9. L Adam Beck, *Oriental Philosophy*, 1928, N.Y.
10. Chang Chen Chi, *The Practice of Zen*, 1959, N.Y.
11. *Tao. The Great Luminant*, translated by Evan Morgan, 1933.
12. The *Way of Life*, Lao-tzu, translated by R B. Blakney, 1955, N.Y.
13. L. Adam Beck, *The Story of Oriental Philosophy* 1928. N.Y.
14. *The Book of Tao*, translated by F.J. MacHovec, 1962.
15. Lao Tzu, *Tao Te Ching: A Way of Life*, R. B. Blakney, N.Y.
16. Eric Hoffer *The Passionate State of Mind*, 1954, N.Y.
17. Ibid.
18. *Loong* is the English phonetic of the Cantonese word Leung, which means "dragon." (Bruce Lee's Chinese nickname was Lee Siu Leung, or Lee Little Dragon.)
19. Alan Watts, *The Way of Zen*.
20. L. Adam Beck, *Oriental Philosophy*, 1928, N.Y.
21. Chang Chen Chi, *The Practice of Zen*.
22. *Introduction to Saint Thomas Aquinas*, edited by Anton C. Pegis (New York-Modern Library, 1948).
23. From Bruce Lee's handwritten notes entitled "Commentaries on the Martial Way," vol. I. Bruce Lee Papers.

24. From Bruce Lee's handwritten note from his notes for *The Silent Flute*, circa 1970. Bruce Lee Papers.
25. *Note:* It is unlikely that this was Lee's choice of title, as in the essay he is speaking of all martial artists who are bound by tradition and not just one segment, that is, karate practitioners.
26. *Note:* Bruce Lee wrote "Expand!" in the margin next to this sentence, indicating a reminder to himself to elaborate on this point at some unspecified time in the future.
27. *Note:* *The Big Boss* was the name of Bruce Lee's first film for Golden Harvest. It shattered all existing box office records in Hong Kong in 1971. It was later released in North America as *Fist of Fury.*
28. From Steve McQueen quoted in an article entitled "Bruce Lee Touched the Lives of the Greats," published in the *Bruce Lee Memorial*, and *Blackbelt Magazine's Best of Bruce Lee #2*, © 1975, Rainbow Publications.
29. *Note:* Pearl Tso and, indeed, the entire Tso family were close friends of Bruce Lee's family when he lived in Hong Kong during the 1950s, and they remained friends throughout the remainder of Bruce Lee's life.
30. *Note:* Taky Kimura was one of Bruce Lee's closest friends and the assistant instructor of Bruce Lee's Seattle *kwoon.*
31. *Note:* T'ai Kik is the Cantonese pronunciation of the Mandarin T'ai Chi, the internal martial arts system known in the West as t'ai chi ch'uan. T'ai Kik also refers to the Yin-Yang symbol. Please see Bruce Lee's explanation of this symbol in the essay entitled "Yin-Yang" found in Part Two of this book.
32. *Note:* Jhoon Rhee is considered the "Father of tae kwon do in North America," and he was a close friend of Bruce Lee's.
33. *Note:* Larry Hartsell was a student of Bruce Lee's from Lee's Los Angeles Chinatown school.
34. *Note:* "John" (last name uncertain) was a friend of Bruce Lee's who had written to Lee, circa 1972.

Index

The family of Bruce Lee wishes to acknowledge:

The dedication of John Little, whose passion for the art and philosophy of Bruce Lee has inspired this publication, and who has spent hours researching, studying, annotating, and organizing Bruce's prolific writings, photos, and memorabilia and gathering the recollection of friends and students.

And, Adrian Marshall, attorney for the estate of Bruce Lee for nearly thirty years, who, with caring attention to the best interests of his friend Bruce Lee, has been instrumental in the publication of this series.

Artist of Life

TO THE READER

The Tuttle Publishing Bruce Lee Library Series is produced in association with the Bruce Lee Foundation, a 501(c)(3) Public Charity based in Los Angeles, California.

The Bruce Lee Foundation is the only not-for-profit organization dedicated to sharing Bruce Lee's insights with the world, by creating opportunities for individuals and applying his message as a personal call to action. They envision a world where Bruce Lee's message and the actions of the Bruce Lee Foundation inspire people to embrace their uniqueness and discover their limitless potential. A portion of proceeds derived from the sale of this book will directly benefit the Bruce Lee Foundation, its programs and the individuals its programs support.

Get Involved:
www.bruceleefoundation.org
www.facebook.com/BruceLeeFoundation
www.twitter.com/BruceLeeFDN
www.instagram.com/BruceLeeFoundation

Contact:
Bruce Lee Foundation
11693 San Vicente Blvd, Ste 918
Los Angeles, CA 90049, USA
info@bruceleefoundation.com

"Books to Span the East and West"

Tuttle Publishing was founded in 1832 in the small New England town of Rutland, Vermont [USA]. Our core values remain as strong today as they were then—to publish best-in-class books which bring people together one page at a time. In 1948, we established a publishing outpost in Japan—and Tuttle is now a leader in publishing English-language books about the arts, languages and cultures of Asia. The world has become a much smaller place today and Asia's economic and cultural influence has grown. Yet the need for meaningful dialogue and information about this diverse region has never been greater. Over the past seven decades, Tuttle has published thousands of books on subjects ranging from martial arts and paper crafts to language learning and literature—and our talented authors, illustrators, designers and photographers have won many prestigious awards. We welcome you to explore the wealth of information available on Asia at **www.tuttlepublishing.com**.